START NOW, PAY LATER

Building a Business with Your
Customers' Money

Haroon Kareem

TheWebPublishersLtd

Copyright © 2024 Haroon Kareem

All rights reserved.
No part of this book may be reproduced, distributed, or transmitted in any form or by any means, including photocopying, recording, or other electronic or mechanical methods, without the prior written permission of the publisher, except in the case of brief quotations embodied in critical reviews and certain other noncommercial uses permitted by copyright law.
Published by TheWebPublishersLtd
This is a work of nonfiction. While the author has made every effort to ensure the accuracy and completeness of the information contained in this book, the author assumes no responsibility for errors or omissions. The advice and strategies contained herein may not be suitable for your situation. You should consult with a professional where appropriate. The author shall not be held liable for any damages arising from the use of this book.
First Edition: 2024

Dedication

To all the dreamers and doers who dared to believe that they could build something extraordinary from nothing.
To those who trusted themselves, trusted their customers, and trusted the journey, even when the path was uncertain.
This book is for you—the resilient, the determined, the ones who see opportunity in every challenge.
May your courage to start small lead you to achieve greatness.

CONTENTS

Title Page
Copyright
Dedication
Introduction
Chapter 1: The New Entrepreneurial Mindset ... 1
Chapter 2: Lean Beginnings – Starting with What You Have ... 8
Chapter 3: The Customer is Your Investor ... 13
Chapter 4: The First Step – Identifying a Customer-Funded Business Idea ... 18
Chapter 5: Validating Your Idea Without Spending Money ... 24
Chapter 6: Pre-Selling Your Product – Making Money Before You Build ... 30
Chapter 7: Crowdfunding – Let Your Customers Fund Your Big Idea ... 36
Chapter 8: Subscriptions, Memberships, and Early-Bird Deals ... 42
Chapter 9: Building Your Product or Service with Limited Resources ... 48
Chapter 10: Creating a Brand That Customers Love ... 53
Chapter 11: Marketing on a Shoestring Budget ... 59
Chapter 12: Using Customer Revenue to Scale Your Business ... 65
Chapter 13: Turning Customers into Advocates and Brand Ambassadors ... 71

Chapter 14: Leveraging Customer Feedback to Drive Innovation — 77

Chapter 15: Staying Profitable Without Taking on Debt or Investors — 83

Chapter 16: Building a Business That Can Thrive in Any Economy — 88

Epilogue — 95

Afterword — 97

Acknowledgement — 99

About The Author — 101

INTRODUCTION

The $30 Startup Myth
The idea that you need a significant amount of money to start a business is one of the most pervasive myths in the entrepreneurial world. It's the reason many dreams are shelved before they even have the chance to begin. How often have you heard someone say, "I'd love to start my own business, but I don't have the money"? It's a common belief that in order to succeed, you need investors, loans, or deep pockets. But what if I told you that you could start a business with as little as $30? That's right—$30. And not only start, but also grow that business into something sustainable, profitable, and scalable.

Why the Idea That You Need a Lot of Money to Start a Business Is a Myth
The truth is, most successful businesses don't start with a large investment. Many of the most iconic companies we know today started on shoestring budgets. What they had in abundance, however, was creativity, determination, and a customer-focused mindset. You don't need millions to launch your dream; what you need is an understanding of how to use your first customers to fund your growth.

Money is, of course, an important part of running a business, but you don't need a lot of it to get started. What you truly need is the ability to solve a problem, provide value, and deliver something that people are willing to pay for. When you focus on those essentials, you can start with almost nothing. The first few dollars you earn can then be reinvested to grow your business step by step. This is what I call the "customer-funded model."

A Brief Introduction to the Customer-Funded Model and Why It

Works

The customer-funded model flips the traditional business funding model on its head. Rather than securing investment first and then building a product, the customer-funded approach focuses on getting customers first and using their money to build and scale the business. It's a simple concept, but it's extremely powerful.

Here's why it works:

1.
Immediate Cash Flow: From day one, you're generating revenue from real customers, not relying on external funding or accumulating debt. This makes the business sustainable from the start.

2.
Validation: By pre-selling or getting early commitments from customers, you're validating your product idea. This minimizes the risk of spending time and money building something that no one wants.

3.
Control: You don't need to give up equity or take on debt. This means you retain full control over your business, and you can grow it at your own pace.

4.
Customer-Driven Innovation: Because your customers are funding your business, you can continually gather feedback and improve your product or service to meet their needs, ensuring a better fit and long-term success.

The customer-funded model isn't just about generating cash; it's about creating a sustainable, customer-centric business. It empowers you to start small, iterate based on feedback, and scale without needing to seek traditional investment.

My Personal Story: How I Started My Own Business with Minimal Capital

I know this model works because I've lived it. When I started my business, I had only 799 Indian Rupees. I was just 16 years old and passionate about coding. With that small amount of money,

I bought a domain and used free hosting to launch a website that offered coding training online. I didn't even have the syllabus ready when my first customer paid me 8,100 Indian Rupees for the course. I used that money to buy my first webcam to start delivering live lessons.

From there, everything grew step by step, using the revenue generated from my customers to build and scale the business. I didn't rely on external investors or loans—I let my customers fund my growth. That small investment of 799 Rupees became the foundation of my business, proving that you don't need a lot of money to get started. All you need is the ability to create value for your customers and the determination to keep pushing forward.

What You'll Learn in This Book

This book is for aspiring entrepreneurs who are ready to take action but feel held back by the belief that they need more money to get started. In "Start Now, Pay Later: Building a Business with Your Customers' Money," you'll learn exactly how to:

- Start a business with minimal capital: Whether you have $30 or $300, you'll discover how to use what you already have to launch a business and generate your first sales.

- Leverage the customer-funded model: I'll show you how to get your customers to pay for your product or service before you even build it, providing the cash flow you need to grow without taking on debt or giving up equity.

- Pre-sell your idea: You'll learn step-by-step strategies for pre-selling your product or service, generating revenue before you even launch, and validating your business idea in the process.

- Market on a budget: I'll teach you how to attract customers and drive sales using low-cost or free marketing strategies, so you can grow your business without burning through your limited resources.

-

Build a profitable, scalable business: You'll learn how to reinvest customer revenue to expand your business, all while staying lean and adaptable. This book will guide you through the process of scaling your business without ever needing traditional investors. Each chapter is packed with actionable advice, real-world examples, and practical tools that you can start using immediately. Whether you're just starting out or looking to take your business to the next level, the strategies in this book will help you build a business that grows with customer money—without the stress of seeking loans or investments.

Now is the time to rethink how businesses can be built. You don't need investors. You don't need a huge bank account. What you need is the drive to start now and the understanding of how to make your customers your greatest investors. Let's get started.

CHAPTER 1: THE NEW ENTREPRENEURIAL MINDSET

When I was 16, I had an idea. It wasn't a fully formed business plan or a groundbreaking invention—just a simple idea. I had a passion for coding, and I wanted to teach others. But there was one problem: I only had 799 Indian Rupees in my pocket. That's not even $30. To most people, it would seem impossible to start a business with such a small amount of money. After all, don't you need big investments to get a business off the ground? Don't you need loans, or investors, or deep pockets to make it work? That's what most people think.

But that's not how I saw it.

With that 799 Rupees, I bought a domain name and set up free hosting. I didn't have a product yet—no curriculum, no teaching materials. All I had was the determination to make something happen. I created a simple website offering online coding lessons. I didn't even know how I was going to deliver the lessons, but I trusted that if I could get people interested, I'd figure it out. Then, something incredible happened. Before I even finished creating the lessons, I received my first payment. One customer paid me 8,100 Rupees, enough to buy my first webcam and start delivering live lessons. That moment changed everything for me. I realized I didn't need a massive investment to start a business. What I needed was trust—trust in my skills, trust in my idea, and trust in my customers. They didn't just buy my product; they funded my business.

Why Most People Believe You Need Big Investments to Start a Business

It's easy to see why so many people believe you need a lot of money to start a business. We're constantly bombarded with stories of startups raising millions of dollars in funding before they even have a product to sell. Entrepreneurs pitch their ideas to venture capitalists, angel investors, and banks, hoping to secure enough capital to bring their ideas to life. The headlines are full of stories about businesses that raised massive amounts of money and grew seemingly overnight. It creates the perception that without big financial backing, starting a business is nearly impossible.

This mindset comes from a few key beliefs:

1. The Fear of Competition: Many aspiring entrepreneurs believe they need a lot of money to compete with established businesses. They think they need to match the marketing budgets,

infrastructure, and product offerings of their competitors from day one. The idea of starting small seems like an invitation to be crushed by bigger, better-funded companies.

2. The Safety Net of Investment: There's also a belief that securing a big investment provides a safety net. If the business struggles or fails, the founder isn't risking their own money—they're using someone else's. This leads people to prioritize finding investors or loans over finding customers, which can be a dangerous mindset.

3. The Desire for Perfection: Many new entrepreneurs want to create the "perfect" product or service before they launch. They feel like they need a lot of money to build something flawless right from the start. In reality, this pursuit of perfection can delay progress and increase the financial risk.

But here's the truth: You don't need a big investment to start a business. In fact, starting small and relying on your customers to fund your growth can be one of the most powerful ways to build a sustainable, successful company.

Shifting from Traditional Funding to Customer-Funded Growth

When I received that first payment from my customer, I realized something crucial: I didn't need to rely on traditional funding sources. I didn't need to take out a loan or give up equity to an investor. My customers could be my investors. They provided the money I needed to grow, and they validated my idea in the process.

This is what I call customer-funded growth—the idea that you can start small, generate revenue from your first customers, and use that revenue to build and scale your business. It's a model that's much more sustainable and less risky than relying on outside capital. And the best part? You stay in control. You don't have to answer to investors or worry about repaying loans.

Here's how I made that shift in my own mindset:

1. Focusing on Customers, Not Investors: I stopped thinking about how I could attract investors and started thinking about how I

could attract customers. I realized that if I could deliver value to my customers, they would fund my business. This shift allowed me to focus on solving real problems for real people, rather than pitching hypothetical ideas to investors.

2. Starting Small and Iterating: I didn't need to create a perfect product from the beginning. Instead, I started with a minimal viable product (MVP)—in my case, simple coding lessons—and improved it as I went along. I used the feedback and payments from my customers to refine and expand my offering.

3. Building Trust with Customers: I learned to trust my customers to guide my business decisions. Their payments were proof that I was on the right track, and their feedback helped me improve. This trust was mutual—I trusted them to fund my business, and they trusted me to deliver value.

How I Built Confidence in Myself and Trusted My Customers

In those early days, it wasn't easy to have confidence. I was young, inexperienced, and starting with almost no money. But that first payment from a customer gave me a huge boost in confidence. It wasn't just about the money; it was about the validation. Someone believed in my idea enough to pay for it before it was even fully built.

Over time, as more customers came on board, my confidence grew. I realized that I didn't need to rely on anyone else to fund my business. My customers believed in me, and that was enough. The more I trusted my customers, the more they trusted me, and the business began to grow organically.

One of the most important lessons I learned was that confidence comes from taking action. If I had waited until I had a perfect product or a big investment, I might never have started. But by taking small steps—buying a domain, offering basic lessons, and gradually improving—I built the confidence to keep going.

Real-World Examples of Customer-Funded Businesses

I'm not the only one who's built a business this way. Many successful entrepreneurs have started with little capital and grown through customer funding. Here are a couple of examples that demonstrate the power of the customer-funded model:

1. Sara Blakely – Spanx: Sara Blakely started Spanx with just $5,000 in savings. She didn't seek outside investment; instead, she focused on creating a product that solved a real problem for her customers. By selling directly to consumers, she used the revenue from her first sales to grow the business. Spanx is now a billion-dollar company.

2. Basecamp – Jason Fried and David Heinemeier Hansson: Basecamp, a project management tool, started as a side project. The founders didn't take on any outside investment. Instead, they built a simple product and sold it to customers. Over time, they reinvested the profits into growing the business, and today, Basecamp is one of the most successful project management tools in the world.

These examples, like my own story, show that customer-funded growth is a powerful way to build a business. It allows you to stay in control, reduce risk, and grow sustainably.

Key Takeaways:

• You don't need a big investment to start; you need belief and action. Trust in your abilities, your ideas, and the value you can offer to your customers.

• Trust that your customers can be your best investors. They will not only provide the revenue you need to grow but also validate your business idea and guide your development.

• Confidence grows when you shift focus from needing funds to serving your customers. Taking small, consistent steps will build the confidence you need to succeed.

Starting with just 799 Rupees may have seemed impossible, but it wasn't. By trusting my skills, serving my customers, and letting their payments fund my growth, I was able to build a business without ever relying on loans or investors. And if I could do it, so can you.

The journey of building a business doesn't begin with a large investment; it begins with a mindset. A mindset that prioritizes customers over investors, action over perfection, and trust over fear. You don't need to wait for the perfect time or the perfect amount of money. Start small, trust your customers, and let them help you grow.

CHAPTER 2: LEAN BEGINNINGS – STARTING WITH WHAT YOU HAVE

After that first customer paid me, I realized something important: starting small doesn't mean thinking small. In fact, starting small was what gave me the freedom to experiment, grow, and find my footing as an entrepreneur. I didn't rush to create a full platform with all the bells and whistles. I wasn't trying to compete with the big players right away. Instead, I focused on what I had: my coding skills, a simple website, and the ability to offer personalized one-on-one lessons.

It was far from glamorous, but it worked. My customer base began growing slowly, one student at a time. And each time I earned money from a new student, I reinvested it into the business. But I was careful not to spend more than I earned. Instead of splurging on expensive marketing campaigns or hiring a team, I relied on free tools like social media to attract more students. I used the profits from my early sales to buy better equipment and improve my lessons bit by bit.

This was a critical lesson for me: starting with what you have doesn't limit your future. It just gives you a chance to build something solid from the ground up. You don't need to wait until you have everything perfectly in place to start. You just need to take that first step and make the most of what you have.

Starting with What You Have Doesn't Limit Your Future

It's easy to fall into the trap of thinking you need everything to be perfect before you can start a business. You might feel like you need the latest technology, a fancy website, or a huge marketing budget. But the truth is, none of that is necessary in the beginning. What's far more important is your ability to identify what you have and use it to create value for your customers.

For me, it was my coding knowledge. I didn't have the money to build a full-scale online education platform, but I did have the skills to teach people one-on-one. So, I focused on delivering value through personal interactions. I offered simple coding lessons and tutoring, and it worked because I was solving a real problem for my customers.

Many entrepreneurs make the mistake of thinking they need to wait for the perfect moment or gather more resources before they start. But if you wait for perfect conditions, you might never begin. By starting small and leveraging what you already have, you can learn, grow, and refine your business over time.

Here's the key: small beginnings don't limit big dreams. In fact, they are often the best way to build a strong foundation for future growth.

How I Identified the Strengths, Resources, and Skills I Had to Create Something Valuable

Looking back, I realize that identifying and leveraging my strengths was one of the most important steps in building my business. At first, I didn't have much—just 799 Indian Rupees, my coding skills, and a lot of determination. But I knew that if I could use those skills to help others, I'd be able to create value and build something that people would pay for.

So, I asked myself a few key questions:

- What skills do I already have?
- What problems can I solve for people using those skills?
- What resources are available to me that don't require a lot of money?
- How can I get my first few customers with minimal investment?

By focusing on my strengths and the resources I had, I was able to take action right away. I didn't need to spend thousands of Rupees on a polished product. I just needed to solve a problem for my customers and deliver value through the tools I had available.

Practical Tips for Using Free or Low-Cost Tools to Get Started

One of the most powerful lessons I learned is that you don't need a lot of money to start marketing your business. Thanks to the internet, there are countless free or low-cost tools that can help you get started and build a customer base. Here are some of the tools I used to grow my business without spending a fortune:

1. Social Media: Social media platforms like Facebook, Instagram, and LinkedIn were instrumental in helping me reach potential students. I didn't need to pay for ads right away—I simply posted valuable content related to coding, shared free tips, and engaged with my audience. Over time, this helped me build a community of people who were interested in learning from me.

2. Email Marketing: Once I started getting more students, I began building an email list. I used free email marketing tools to send out newsletters, tips, and updates about my courses. This kept my students engaged and helped me attract more business through word of mouth.

3. Website Builders: In the beginning, I didn't need a fancy, expensive website. I used a free website builder and focused on creating a simple, easy-to-navigate site where people could learn about my services and contact me for lessons. As my business grew, I reinvested in upgrading the website.

4. Content Marketing: I started a blog to share coding tips and tutorials. This not only showcased my expertise but also helped attract students who were looking for free resources. By offering valuable content, I was able to build trust with potential students and convert them into paying customers over time.

By using these free or low-cost tools, I was able to grow my business without breaking the bank. The key was focusing on delivering value first, and the money followed.

Stories of Entrepreneurs Who Used What They Had to Build Something Great

I'm not the only one who started small and grew through resourcefulness. Here are a couple of stories of entrepreneurs who used what they had to build something great:

1. Sara Blakely – Spanx: Sara Blakely started Spanx with just $5,000 in savings. She didn't have any experience in fashion or manufacturing, but she had an idea for a product that solved a real problem for women. Instead of waiting for more funding or experience, she used her savings to create the first prototype and personally pitched it to retailers. Spanx is now a billion-dollar company, and Blakely is one of the world's most successful entrepreneurs—all because she started small with what she had.

2. Jason Fried & David Heinemeier Hansson – Basecamp: Basecamp, a project management tool, started as a side project. The founders didn't have a huge budget, but they built a simple tool that solved a real problem for their customers. They focused on delivering value through simplicity, and over time, they reinvested profits to improve and scale the product. Today, Basecamp is used by thousands of teams worldwide.

These stories show that starting small doesn't limit your potential. What matters is how you use the resources and skills you have to create something valuable.

Key Takeaways:

• You don't need fancy tools or large investments to start; use what's available to you. Free tools like social media, email marketing, and website builders are enough to get started. The most important thing is delivering value.

• Focus on offering value first, and the money will follow. By solving a problem and delivering a product or service that people need, you can start generating revenue without a huge upfront investment.

• Small, consistent efforts lead to long-term growth. Starting small doesn't mean you'll stay small. By reinvesting your earnings, using free tools, and delivering value, you can gradually scale your business and achieve big results.

Starting with what you have is one of the most empowering decisions you can make as an entrepreneur. Don't wait for the perfect conditions. Use the tools and skills you already have, solve a problem, and take action. Success doesn't come from having everything in place; it comes from making the most of what you've got and building from there.

CHAPTER 3: THE CUSTOMER IS YOUR INVESTOR

The day I received that first payment, everything changed. It wasn't just the money itself—though that 8,100 Rupees was certainly welcome. It was the realization that my customers could fund my business. I didn't need to rely on investors or loans; I could rely on the people who believed in what I had to offer. They weren't just buying a product or service—they were investing in me. That payment wasn't just cash; it was validation that my idea had value.

With that first payment, I immediately reinvested in my business. I used the money to buy a webcam, improving the quality of my coding lessons. It wasn't a huge upgrade, but it made a difference. As more students signed up for my lessons, I listened to their feedback. They told me what they liked, what they didn't, and what could be improved. Their feedback was as valuable as their money, helping me refine and enhance my offering. This was the power of customer funding—not just financial capital, but insight, validation, and the opportunity to grow based on real-world needs.

The Power of Customer Funding

When people talk about starting a business, they often focus on raising money from outside investors—venture capitalists, angel investors, or even banks. They imagine needing a big chunk of cash upfront to build their product, hire staff, and launch a marketing campaign. But customer funding flips that model upside down.

In the customer-funded model, your first customers provide both the capital and the validation you need to grow. Instead of relying on investors to bet on your potential success, you get paid by people who are already invested in the value you're offering. This is a more sustainable and organic way to build a business because:

1. You Stay in Control: When you take money from outside investors, you often give up control—whether that's equity in your company or decision-making power. But when your customers fund your business, you remain in control. You get to set the direction, pace, and priorities of your company.

2. You Minimize Risk: Taking on debt or giving up equity can be risky, especially for new entrepreneurs. But with customer funding, you reduce financial risk. You're not taking on loans that need to be repaid, and you're not beholden to investors. Instead, you're using revenue from customers to fuel your growth.

3. You Validate Your Idea Early: Every time a customer pays you, they're validating your business idea. They're telling you, "Yes, this is worth paying for." That's invaluable feedback, especially in the early stages of a business. You don't have to guess whether your idea will work—you have proof from people willing to pay for it.

4. You Can Pivot Based on Real Feedback: Because your customers are both your investors and your source of feedback, you can pivot and adjust your offering based on what they want. Instead of building a product in isolation, you're constantly improving based on real-world input.

How Customers Provide Both Capital and Feedback

When I received that first payment, I immediately reinvested the money into improving my lessons. The webcam I purchased wasn't fancy, but it allowed me to deliver a better experience for my students. More importantly, as I gained more customers, I realized that their feedback was just as important as their money. They were helping me shape the future of my business.

I started to see every new customer as both an investor and an advisor. Their payments gave me the cash flow I needed to grow, but their feedback gave me the insight I needed to improve. It was a cycle of growth: the more customers I served, the more feedback I received, and the more I could refine my offering to meet their needs.

One student, for example, told me that they wanted more advanced coding tutorials. I hadn't planned on offering that level of detail initially, but because of the feedback, I started developing more complex lessons. Another student suggested that I offer downloadable materials to complement the live lessons, which led me to create supplementary guides and exercises.

This ongoing feedback loop became one of the most valuable aspects of customer funding. Not only did I get paid to develop my product, but I was also given a clear roadmap for improvement based on what my customers actually wanted.

The Importance of Building Strong Relationships with Customers Early

As I continued to grow my business, I learned something crucial: strong relationships with customers are the foundation of any successful business. When you treat your customers as investors —people who are helping to fund and shape your business— you build a sense of loyalty and trust that goes far beyond the transaction.

In the early days, I made it a point to get to know each of my students personally. I'd check in with them after each lesson, asking what they found useful and what could be improved. I'd send follow-up emails with tips and additional resources, ensuring that they felt supported. This not only helped me improve my lessons but also built a loyal customer base. Many of my early students referred their friends and colleagues to me, and my business grew largely through word of mouth.

These relationships were the bedrock of my success. My customers weren't just paying for a service—they were part of a community I was building. They were invested in my success because I was invested in theirs. This is the power of customer funding: when you focus on serving your customers well, they'll fund your growth, refer new business, and help you refine your product along the way.

Case Studies of Businesses That Thrived by Putting Customers First

There are countless examples of businesses that have thrived by treating their customers as investors and putting their needs first. Here are two stories that illustrate the power of customer funding:

1. Buffer – The Social Media Management Tool: Buffer, a popular social media management tool, started with a simple idea: help people schedule and manage their social media posts. But instead of raising money from investors upfront, the founders, Joel Gascoigne and Leo Widrich, built a minimal viable product (MVP) and launched it to a small group of users. They used the revenue from their early customers to fund further development, listening carefully to feedback and improving the tool based on user needs. Today, Buffer is used by millions of people and businesses around the world—all without raising significant outside funding in the early stages.

2. MVMT Watches – Jake Kassan and Kramer LaPlante: MVMT, a direct-to-consumer watch brand, started with little more than a passion for design and a small crowdfunding campaign. Instead of seeking traditional investors, the founders used platforms like Indiegogo to pre-sell their watches and raise the money they needed to start production. Their customers essentially funded

the company's growth, and their feedback helped shape future designs and product lines. Today, MVMT is a globally recognized brand, and it all started with customer funding.

Key Takeaways:

• Your customers are your best investors; they provide both cash and insight. Every time a customer pays for your product or service, they're validating your business idea and helping fund your growth.

• Build strong relationships early and let customer feedback guide your growth. When you listen to your customers and treat them as partners in your success, they'll provide the roadmap for improvement and help you build loyalty.

• Customer validation is more important than investment capital. The best way to prove that your business works is to get paying customers. Their willingness to spend money on your product is the best validation you can get.

By treating my customers as investors, I was able to grow my business without relying on outside capital. Their payments gave me the cash flow I needed, and their feedback helped me refine and improve my offering. This customer-funded model not only reduced my financial risk but also allowed me to stay in control of my business, growing at a pace that made sense for me and my customers. If you focus on delivering value and building strong relationships with your customers, they will be your most valuable partners in success.

CHAPTER 4: THE FIRST STEP – IDENTIFYING A CUSTOMER-FUNDED BUSINESS IDEA

When I started my business, I didn't have a grand plan. I didn't spend months—or even weeks—trying to come up with the "perfect" idea. I knew people needed help learning how to code, and I had the skills to teach them. It was as simple as that. I wasn't aiming to revolutionize the tech education industry or create something that had never been done before. I just wanted to solve a problem for a specific group of people who needed what I could offer.

My first few clients were small, but they were real. Their willingness to pay for my lessons showed me that there was real demand for what I was offering. That early validation was crucial—it wasn't a hunch or a guess, it was proof that my idea had legs. The beauty of this approach was that I didn't need a perfect product to start. I just needed to get out there, offer my skills, and see how people responded. Their feedback and their payments guided the next steps of my business.

How to Choose a Business Idea That Can Be Customer-Funded from Day One

One of the biggest hurdles for aspiring entrepreneurs is choosing the "right" business idea. Too often, people believe they need to come up with something revolutionary or create a product that's completely unique. But the truth is, most successful businesses don't start with groundbreaking ideas. They start by solving real problems for real people.

When you're choosing a business idea that can be customer-funded from day one, the most important thing to focus on is value. What problem are you solving? Who needs that problem solved, and are they willing to pay for it? The clearer you are about these answers, the easier it will be to create a customer-funded business model.

Here's how to identify an idea that can be funded by customers from the very beginning:

1. Solve a Real Problem: Instead of trying to create something revolutionary, focus on a problem that already exists. What are people struggling with, and how can you help solve that problem? In my case, I knew that people wanted to learn how to code but didn't always have access to personalized instruction. I offered my skills as a solution, and people were willing to pay for it.

2. Start with What You Know: You don't need to reinvent the wheel. Start by looking at the skills, resources, and experiences you already have. What can you offer that others would find valuable? For me, it was my coding skills. I didn't need to learn something new or acquire new resources; I just needed to package what I already knew in a way that solved a problem for my clients.

3. Look for Immediate Demand: You want to find a business idea that has immediate demand—something that people need right now, not something that might be in demand someday. The beauty of a customer-funded business is that it allows you to start small and grow based on real-world feedback. The sooner you can get customers paying for your product or service, the better.

4. Test Your Idea Quickly: Once you have an idea, don't spend too much time refining or perfecting it. The goal is to get out there, offer your product or service, and see if people are willing to pay for it. You don't need a fully built business to start—just a simple

way to test your idea and get feedback from potential customers.

Identifying Products or Services That Customers Will Pay for Before They're Fully Built

One of the key elements of a customer-funded business model is that you don't need to build a fully developed product before you start making money. In fact, many successful businesses start by pre-selling their product or offering a service before it's fully built. This allows you to generate revenue and validate your idea at the same time, reducing the risk of building something no one wants.

In my case, I didn't have a fully developed curriculum when I started offering coding lessons. I had a basic framework, but I was able to start teaching and refine the curriculum as I went. My customers paid me before I had everything completely built, which gave me the cash flow I needed to keep improving the product.

Here's how you can identify products or services that customers will pay for before they're fully built:

1. Pre-Sell Your Product or Service: One of the simplest ways to generate revenue before you've fully developed your offering is to pre-sell it. This works especially well for digital products, courses, or services. You offer customers the chance to buy in early, often at a discount or with added value, and use that revenue to fund the development of your product. Not only does this give you the money you need to build, but it also validates your idea.

2. Offer a Minimum Viable Product (MVP): An MVP is the simplest version of your product or service that still delivers value to your customers. It doesn't need to be perfect or fully built—it just needs to solve a problem. Once you have customers paying for your MVP, you can use their feedback and payments to improve and expand your offering.

3. Focus on High-Value, Low-Cost Solutions: Your goal in the beginning is to deliver value without overinvesting in

development. Look for ways to offer high-value solutions that don't require a lot of upfront capital. In my case, I offered personalized coding lessons, which didn't require any additional investment beyond my time and expertise. This allowed me to start generating revenue immediately without having to build anything expensive.

Finding a Niche That Allows You to Start Small and Scale Over Time

Starting small doesn't mean thinking small. In fact, one of the best ways to build a successful business is by starting with a specific niche that allows you to grow gradually over time. When I started, I wasn't trying to offer coding lessons to everyone—I focused on a small group of people who needed personalized instruction. This allowed me to start with a manageable number of clients and refine my offering as I went.

By focusing on a niche, you can:

1. Start Small and Validate Quickly: When you focus on a specific audience with a specific problem, it's easier to validate your idea. You can test your product or service with a small group of people, gather feedback, and make adjustments before expanding.

2. Build a Loyal Customer Base: When you focus on serving a specific group of people, you can build strong relationships and loyalty. Your customers will feel like you truly understand their needs, and they'll be more likely to recommend your business to others.

3. Scale as You Grow: Once you've validated your idea and built a loyal customer base, you can gradually expand your offering. This might mean adding new products, serving a larger audience, or moving into new markets. But by starting with a niche, you reduce the risk of spreading yourself too thin in the early stages.

Examples of Businesses Across Industries That Used Customer-

Funded Models

Customer-funded business models aren't limited to one industry. Many successful businesses across different sectors have started small and grown through customer funding. Here are two examples that show how versatile this model can be:

1. **The $100 Startup – Chris Guillebeau:** Chris Guillebeau's book The $100 Startup profiles dozens of entrepreneurs who started businesses with little to no capital and grew through customer funding. One of the standout examples is Brett Kelly, who wrote Evernote Essentials, a guide to using the Evernote app. Brett pre-sold his book to early customers before it was fully written, using their payments to finish the project. This allowed him to generate revenue and validate his idea before investing too much time or money.

2. **Pebble – The Smartwatch Pioneer:** Pebble, one of the first successful smartwatches, started with a crowdfunding campaign on Kickstarter. Instead of building the product first, the founders created a prototype and pitched it to potential customers. They raised over $10 million from early supporters, who essentially pre-ordered the watch before it was fully developed. Pebble used the funds to manufacture the product, proving that customer funding can work even for physical products.

Key Takeaways:

• Focus on solving a specific problem for a specific audience. You don't need to have a revolutionary idea to start a business. Find a problem, offer a solution, and test it with real customers.

• You don't need the perfect idea to start; test what works. Start with what you know and what you can offer immediately. Don't wait for perfection—get your product or service out there and let your customers guide you.

• Start with a niche and expand as your customers guide you. By focusing on a specific audience, you can validate your idea quickly, build loyalty, and scale over time based on real feedback and demand.

Starting a customer-funded business doesn't require a perfect idea or a massive plan. It requires action. Identify a problem, offer a solution, and let your customers validate your idea with their payments and feedback. As you grow, you'll learn, refine, and expand—but it all starts with taking that first step and offering what you have right now.

CHAPTER 5: VALIDATING YOUR IDEA WITHOUT SPENDING MONEY

Before I spent hours developing a detailed curriculum for my coding lessons, I needed to know whether people would actually pay for them. It didn't make sense to pour time and resources into something if there wasn't any real demand. So, instead of diving headfirst into content creation, I decided to test the waters. I reached out to potential students, offered free consultations, and gauged their interest. Their responses made it clear: I was on the right track. But I didn't rush to build everything at once. Instead, I built my lessons step by step, using feedback from these early conversations to shape my offering.

I didn't invest more than I had at any point during this process. I let my customers guide me, and only when I was confident that they wanted what I was offering did I start to refine and expand. This process of validation was essential—it saved me time, money, and the frustration of building something no one wanted. The beauty of this approach was that it didn't cost me anything to validate my idea, but it gave me everything I needed to move forward with confidence.

The Importance of Validating Your Business Idea Before You Invest

One of the biggest mistakes entrepreneurs make is building a product or service without validating the idea first. They spend months—or even years—developing something they think people will want, only to find out that there's no real demand. By the time they launch, they've spent all their resources on something that doesn't resonate with customers.

Validating your business idea before you invest a significant amount of time or money is crucial. It's the difference between guessing and knowing. When you validate your idea, you're gathering real-world data that shows whether people are willing to pay for what you're offering. It's not about building the perfect product from day one—it's about testing your idea with real customers, getting feedback, and making adjustments before you commit too many resources.

How to Validate Your Idea Without Spending Money

The great thing about validating a business idea is that it doesn't have to cost a lot of money. In fact, many of the best validation techniques are free or very low cost. Here's how I validated my coding lessons, and how you can do the same with your business idea:

1. Talk to Potential Customers: The simplest and most effective way to validate your idea is to talk to potential customers. Before I created my detailed coding curriculum, I reached out to people who were interested in learning to code. I offered them free consultations to understand their needs and see if my solution would resonate with them. These conversations were invaluable. They helped me understand what people were looking for, what challenges they were facing, and how I could position my lessons to meet those needs.

How you can do it: Reach out to your target audience and start a conversation. Ask them about their pain points, what solutions they're currently using, and whether they'd be interested in what you're offering. You don't need a polished product to have these conversations—just a clear idea of what problem you're trying to solve.

2. Use Social Media to Test Interest: Social media is a powerful tool for validating business ideas. I used platforms like Facebook and LinkedIn to gauge interest in my coding lessons. I posted about my offerings, shared tips and advice, and asked for feedback. The responses helped me understand what people were interested in and what kind of demand there was for my services.

How you can do it: Use social media to ask questions, run polls, or share content related to your business idea. If people engage with your posts and express interest, that's a good sign that there's demand for what you're offering. You can also join groups or forums where your target audience hangs out and see what they're talking about. Are they discussing problems that your product or service could solve? If so, reach out and offer your solution.

3. Run a Simple Survey: Surveys are another great way to validate your idea. I created a simple survey for potential students, asking about their learning preferences, coding experience, and what they were looking for in a coding instructor. This helped me fine-tune my offering and make sure I was addressing real needs.

How you can do it: Create a survey using free tools like Google Forms or SurveyMonkey. Ask questions that help you understand your target audience's needs, preferences, and willingness to pay for a solution. Share the survey on social media, send it to your email list, or post it in relevant online communities. The insights you gather will help you refine your idea and make sure you're building something people actually want.

Building a Minimum Viable Product (MVP)

Once I had validated the demand for my coding lessons, I didn't rush to build a fully developed curriculum. Instead, I started with a Minimum Viable Product (MVP)—the simplest version of my service that still delivered value to my students. I built the lessons as I went, refining them based on feedback from each session. This allowed me to offer real value to my students without over-investing in time or resources upfront.

An MVP is a powerful way to validate your idea while still providing value. It's not about building something perfect; it's about creating a basic version of your product or service that solves a problem for your customers. Once you have that in place, you can gather feedback, make improvements, and gradually build out the full offering.

How to build an MVP:

• Focus on the Core Problem: Your MVP should address the main problem your customers are facing. Don't worry about adding extra features or making it perfect—just focus on delivering the core value.

• Launch Quickly: The sooner you get your MVP into the hands of customers, the sooner you can gather feedback and make improvements. Don't wait for everything to be perfect before you launch.

• Iterate Based on Feedback: Once people start using your MVP, listen to their feedback. What do they like? What could be improved? Use this feedback to refine your offering and make it better over time.

By building an MVP, you're validating your idea in real time. You're not guessing whether people will like it—you're getting real feedback from real customers.

Examples of Businesses That Used Validation Techniques to Avoid Costly Mistakes

Many successful businesses have used validation techniques to avoid costly mistakes and ensure that they're building products people actually want. Here are a couple of examples:

1. Dropbox – Drew Houston: Before Dropbox became the cloud storage giant it is today, its founder Drew Houston needed to

validate the idea. Instead of building a full product from the start, Houston created a simple video explaining how Dropbox would work. He shared the video with potential users and gauged their interest. The response was overwhelmingly positive, which gave Houston the confidence to move forward and build the product. By validating the idea with a simple video, Houston avoided the risk of building a product that no one wanted.

2. Zappos – Tony Hsieh: Zappos, the online shoe retailer, started with a simple MVP. Before building a full e-commerce platform, founder Nick Swinmurn tested the idea by posting photos of shoes from local stores on a basic website. When customers placed an order, Swinmurn would go to the store, buy the shoes, and ship them to the customer. This allowed him to validate the demand for buying shoes online without investing in inventory or infrastructure. Once the idea was validated, Zappos scaled into the massive business it is today.

These examples show that you don't need a fully built product to validate your idea. By testing early and gathering feedback, you can avoid costly mistakes and build something that people actually want.

Key Takeaways:

• Validate your idea by talking to customers first. Before you invest time or money into building your product or service, make sure there's demand. Talk to potential customers, ask questions, and listen to their feedback.

• Build only what's necessary to test your idea; the rest can come later. Start with a Minimum Viable Product (MVP) that solves a core problem for your customers. Once you've validated your idea, you can add more features and build out the full offering.

• Listening to your customers ensures you're building something they actually want. Don't rely on guesswork—use customer feedback to guide your decisions and make sure you're creating a product or service that solves a real problem.

Validating your idea is one of the most important steps in building a successful business. By testing your concept with real customers, gathering feedback, and refining your offering before you invest heavily, you can avoid costly mistakes and build something that people truly want. In the early days of my business, this process saved me time, money, and frustration—and it will do the same for you.

CHAPTER 6: PRE-SELLING YOUR PRODUCT – MAKING MONEY BEFORE YOU BUILD

When I first started offering coding lessons, I didn't have everything ready. In fact, I didn't even have a detailed syllabus or a fully developed teaching plan. What I did have, however, was a clear understanding of what my customers needed and the confidence that I could deliver it. So instead of waiting until I had everything perfectly in place, I started selling the promise of high-quality coding lessons. My first few customers didn't pay for a finished product; they paid for the value I promised to deliver.

This is the power of pre-selling. By selling my services before they were fully built, I was able to generate cash flow right from the start. Those early payments not only gave me the financial breathing room to develop my materials, but they also validated my business idea. I knew that if people were willing to pay upfront, I was on the right track. And because I didn't have to take on debt or seek outside investment, I was able to grow my business organically, reinvesting the money from each new sale to continue building and refining my product.

How to Use Pre-Sales to Raise Money Before Your Business Is Fully

Built

Pre-selling is a powerful strategy for entrepreneurs, especially those working with limited resources. Instead of pouring time and money into building a product before you know if anyone will buy it, pre-selling allows you to gauge interest, generate revenue, and refine your offering based on real customer feedback—all before you've fully built your product or service.

Here's why pre-selling works:

1. It Generates Cash Flow Early: When you pre-sell your product or service, you're getting paid before the product is fully built. This gives you the cash you need to develop the product without going into debt or taking on outside investors. You're essentially using customer payments to fund the creation of your business.

2. It Validates Your Idea: Pre-selling is one of the best ways to validate your business idea. If people are willing to pay for something before it's built, that's a strong indication that there's demand for your product or service. On the other hand, if you struggle to sell pre-orders, it may be a sign that you need to adjust your offer or rethink your business idea.

3. It Builds a Loyal Customer Base Early: When customers pre-order your product, they're not just buying a product—they're investing in your vision. These early supporters often become loyal customers and advocates for your business, helping to spread the word and generate more sales down the road.

Creating Compelling Offers That Customers Are Excited to Buy Early On

The key to a successful pre-sale campaign is creating a compelling offer that gets people excited to buy before your product or service is fully built. People are taking a leap of faith by paying upfront, so you need to give them a reason to trust that the value they'll receive will be worth it.

Here's how to create an offer that resonates with your audience:

1. Highlight the Value: Focus on the value your product or service will provide. Don't just list features; explain how your offering will solve a problem or improve your customers' lives. In my case, I didn't just say I was offering coding lessons—I emphasized that my personalized, one-on-one approach would help my students learn faster and more effectively than traditional classes.

2. Offer Early-Bird Discounts or Bonuses: People love to feel like they're getting a deal, especially when they're taking a risk by pre-ordering something that isn't finished yet. Offering early-bird discounts or exclusive bonuses for pre-order customers can create urgency and incentivize people to buy. For example, I offered my first few students a discounted rate in exchange for their early commitment, and this helped me quickly fill my roster.

3. Build Trust: Since customers are paying before they receive the product, trust is essential. Be transparent about your process, provide regular updates, and make it clear that you're committed to delivering what you've promised. Share testimonials, past work, or any other proof that demonstrates your ability to deliver.

4. Create a Sense of Urgency: Limited-time offers or exclusive spots can create a sense of urgency and encourage people to act quickly. In my case, I only had a limited number of one-on-one tutoring slots available, which created urgency for potential students to book their lessons before the spots were gone.

A Step-by-Step Guide to Running a Pre-Sale Campaign

Running a successful pre-sale campaign takes careful planning and execution. Here's a step-by-step guide to help you get started:

1. Define Your Offer: Before you launch your pre-sale, you need to clearly define what you're offering. This includes outlining the value your product or service will provide, determining the price, and deciding what bonuses or discounts you'll offer to early buyers. Make sure your offer is compelling enough to get people to commit before the product is fully built.

2. Build Anticipation: Before launching your pre-sale, start building anticipation by talking about your product or service on social media, through your email list, or in online communities. Share behind-the-scenes content, teasers, or updates to get people excited about what's coming. The more anticipation you build, the more likely people will be to jump on your pre-sale offer when it goes live.

3. Set Up a Pre-Sale Landing Page: Create a simple landing page where people can learn more about your offer and make their purchase. The landing page should clearly explain the value of your product or service, highlight any early-bird discounts or bonuses, and provide an easy way for customers to make their pre-order. Tools like Leadpages, Shopify, or even a simple WordPress site can be used to set this up quickly and inexpensively.

4. Launch Your Pre-Sale: Once everything is in place, it's time to launch your pre-sale. Send out emails to your list, post on social media, and reach out to potential customers to let them know the pre-sale is live. Make sure to emphasize the limited-time nature of the offer to create urgency.

5. Provide Regular Updates: After customers have made their pre-orders, keep them in the loop with regular updates on the progress of the product. This builds trust and keeps your customers engaged while they're waiting for the final product.

6. Deliver on Your Promises: Once you've collected pre-sale payments, it's crucial to deliver on your promises. Make sure the product or service lives up to the expectations you've set, and be transparent about any delays or changes in the process. Happy pre-sale customers are more likely to become repeat customers and refer others to your business.

Stories of Businesses That Used Pre-Sales to Launch Successfully

Many successful businesses have used pre-sales to generate revenue and validate their ideas before launching. Here are a couple of examples:

1. Kickstarter – The Pebble Watch: The Pebble Watch was one of the most successful pre-sale campaigns of all time. Before the smartwatch was fully built, the founders launched a crowdfunding campaign on Kickstarter to raise money for development. They offered early-bird pricing and exclusive rewards to people who backed the project early. The campaign raised over $10 million in pre-orders, which provided the funding needed to manufacture and ship the watches. Pebble used pre-sales not only to raise money but also to validate the demand for their product.

2. Lean Startup – Eric Ries: In his book The Lean Startup, Eric Ries talks about the importance of validating ideas through pre-sales and customer feedback. He describes how many startups fail because they build products that no one wants. Instead of spending months or years developing a product, Ries advocates for creating a Minimum Viable Product (MVP) and getting customers to buy in early. By pre-selling an MVP, businesses can generate revenue and test their idea before committing to full-scale production.

Key Takeaways:

• You don't need to have a finished product to start making money. Pre-selling allows you to generate revenue before your product or service is fully built, reducing financial risk and providing the cash flow you need to develop your offering.

• Pre-selling gives you both validation and early cash flow. If customers are willing to pay for your product before it's complete, it's a strong sign that there's demand. This validation can help guide your business decisions and give you the confidence to move forward.

• Sell the value of your product or service before it's fully built. Focus on the value you're offering and build trust with your customers by being transparent and delivering on your promises.

Pre-selling is one of the most powerful strategies for launching a business without taking on debt or outside investment. By selling the promise of value before your product is fully built, you can generate early cash flow, validate your idea, and build a loyal customer base—all while reducing financial risk. I used this approach to grow my business from day one, and it's a strategy that can work for you too. The key is to create a compelling offer, build trust with your customers, and deliver on your promises. With pre-sales, you don't need to wait for perfection—you can start making money now, even before your product is finished.

CHAPTER 7: CROWDFUNDING – LET YOUR CUSTOMERS FUND YOUR BIG IDEA

As my business grew and I gained more experience, I began to see the immense power of my customers' willingness to support my ideas before they were fully realized. This wasn't just limited to pre-selling my coding lessons—this idea extended into something much bigger. I watched as other entrepreneurs used crowdfunding platforms like Kickstarter and Indiegogo to raise large amounts of capital by selling a vision of what was to come, not just the final product.

Crowdfunding, I realized, wasn't just about raising money. It was about building a community of people who believed in your idea and were excited to be part of bringing it to life. These platforms gave me the inspiration to think bigger—to take on larger projects and to expand my vision beyond what I could fund through traditional means. The key was understanding that people weren't just buying a product—they were investing in a vision they believed in.

How to Run a Successful Crowdfunding Campaign on Platforms Like Kickstarter or Indiegogo

Crowdfunding has become one of the most popular ways for entrepreneurs to raise money, validate ideas, and build a customer base all at the same time. Platforms like Kickstarter and Indiegogo allow creators to pitch their ideas directly to the public, offering rewards or early access to backers in exchange for their financial support.

Running a successful crowdfunding campaign requires a combination of clear communication, an understanding of what motivates backers, and a well-executed strategy. Here's a breakdown of the key steps to launching a winning crowdfunding campaign:

1. Choose the Right Platform: Not all crowdfunding platforms are created equal. Kickstarter is ideal for creative projects, tech gadgets, and innovative products, while Indiegogo offers more flexibility and allows for both fixed and flexible funding models. Research the platforms to determine which is the best fit for your project and audience.

2. Set Realistic Goals: One of the biggest mistakes new entrepreneurs make is setting funding goals that are too high. It's important to be realistic about how much you need to get started, but also about how much you can reasonably raise. Your goal should cover the costs of bringing your product to market, including manufacturing, marketing, and shipping, but it should also be achievable.

3. Craft a Compelling Story: Crowdfunding isn't just about selling a product—it's about telling a story that resonates with your audience. Why did you create this product? What problem does it solve? How will it make people's lives better? Use storytelling to connect emotionally with your audience and inspire them to support your vision.

4. Offer Irresistible Rewards: Backers on crowdfunding platforms expect to receive something in return for their support. The most common rewards are early access to the product at a discounted price or exclusive items that won't be available later. Make sure your rewards are appealing and aligned with your audience's expectations. Offering different tiers of rewards can

also incentivize backers to pledge more.

5. Create a Great Pitch Video: Your video is one of the most important elements of your crowdfunding campaign. It's your chance to show potential backers who you are, why your product matters, and why they should support you. Keep the video short (around 2-3 minutes), but make sure it covers the key points: who you are, what your product does, and why it's worth backing. A professional-looking video can significantly increase your chances of success.

6. Leverage Social Media and Email Marketing: Your crowdfunding campaign won't succeed if no one knows about it. Use social media and email marketing to get the word out and engage with your audience before, during, and after the campaign. Build excitement around the launch, share updates, and encourage your followers to spread the word.

7. Provide Regular Updates: Once your campaign is live, it's important to keep your backers informed. Share updates on your progress, thank your supporters, and address any questions or concerns they may have. This builds trust and keeps your backers engaged throughout the campaign.

Understanding the Psychology Behind Why People Back Projects

Crowdfunding is not just about selling a product—it's about understanding the motivations behind why people back projects. When someone backs a crowdfunding campaign, they aren't just buying a product or service; they're investing in a vision they believe in. Understanding this psychology can help you craft a more compelling campaign.

Here's why people back crowdfunding projects:

1. They Want to Support Innovation: Many backers are motivated by the desire to support something new and innovative. They like the idea of being part of something that's cutting-edge or disruptive. If your product offers a unique solution to a problem,

emphasize this in your campaign.

2. They Believe in the Creator: People are more likely to back a project if they feel a personal connection to the creator. This is why your story matters so much. Backers want to feel like they're helping someone with a vision bring their dream to life.

3. They Want to Be First: Many backers are excited about the idea of being the first to own or experience a new product. Offering exclusive early access or limited-edition versions of your product can tap into this desire.

4. They Want to Be Part of a Community: Successful crowdfunding campaigns often build a sense of community among backers. When people back a project, they become part of something bigger than themselves. They enjoy the sense of belonging and the opportunity to connect with others who share their interests.

5. They Appreciate Transparency and Updates: Backers want to feel confident that the project they're supporting will succeed. Regular updates and transparency about the process build trust and help backers feel more secure in their decision to support your campaign.

Crafting a Pitch That Resonates with Your Audience

Crafting a compelling pitch is essential to the success of your crowdfunding campaign. Your pitch needs to clearly communicate the value of your product, the vision behind it, and why people should support you. But more than that, it needs to resonate with your audience on an emotional level.

Here's how to craft a pitch that gets people excited:

1. Tell a Story: People connect with stories, not sales pitches. Share the journey behind your product—why did you create it? What challenges did you face along the way? How did you overcome them? This not only makes your campaign more relatable but also helps backers feel personally invested in your success.

2. **Focus on the Problem You're Solving:** Backers want to know how your product will make their lives better. Clearly articulate the problem your product solves and why your solution is unique or better than what's currently available.

3. **Show Your Passion:** Your enthusiasm for your project should shine through in your pitch. Backers are more likely to support you if they see how passionate you are about what you're creating.

4. **Be Transparent About Your Plan:** Backers want to know that you have a solid plan in place for bringing your product to life. Clearly explain how the funds will be used, what your timeline looks like, and how you plan to deliver on your promises.

Real-Life Examples of Crowdfunding Success Stories

There are countless examples of businesses that have used crowdfunding to turn their ideas into reality. Here are two notable examples:

1. **The Pebble Watch:** Pebble's founders turned to Kickstarter to fund their smartwatch, which was one of the first of its kind. They set a goal of raising $100,000, but their campaign took off and raised over $10 million from backers. Pebble offered early access to the watch at discounted prices for backers, creating a sense of urgency and excitement around the launch. The campaign's success not only provided the funding needed to bring the product to market but also helped Pebble build a community of loyal supporters.

2. **Exploding Kittens – The Card Game:** Exploding Kittens, a quirky card game, became one of the most successful crowdfunding campaigns on Kickstarter. The creators set a modest goal of $10,000, but the game's humorous concept and engaging pitch resonated with backers, and they ended up raising over $8 million. The creators kept backers engaged with regular updates, stretch goals, and behind-the-scenes content, which helped build a strong sense of community.

Key Takeaways:

• Crowdfunding allows you to raise money and build a customer base at the same time. It's not just about funding—it's about creating a community of people who believe in your vision and want to see it succeed.

• A strong community is essential for a successful crowdfunding campaign. Engage with your backers, keep them informed, and make them feel like part of your journey.

• People don't just back products; they back visions they believe in. Craft a compelling story around your product and vision, and let your passion shine through. People want to support creators who are passionate, authentic, and transparent.

Crowdfunding is an incredible tool for entrepreneurs who want to bring their big ideas to life without relying on traditional investment. It allows you to raise money, validate your idea, and build a loyal customer base—all while creating a sense of community around your project. By understanding the psychology behind why people back projects and crafting a compelling pitch, you can turn your idea into a reality with the support of your future customers. And in the process, you'll be building more than just a product—you'll be building a brand that people believe in.

CHAPTER 8: SUBSCRIPTIONS, MEMBERSHIPS, AND EARLY-BIRD DEALS

As my business grew, I quickly learned the value of recurring revenue. It wasn't enough to rely on one-off sales, even if they were frequent. What I needed was consistency—a way to predict my income each month so that I could plan for growth. That's when I started offering my clients a subscription-based model for my coding lessons. This shift transformed my business. Not only did it give me a steady stream of cash flow, but it also allowed me to build deeper, more long-term relationships with my clients. They weren't just buying a single lesson; they were investing in ongoing education with me.

At the same time, I experimented with early-bird deals to drive urgency and excitement. Offering discounts to those who signed up early created a sense of scarcity that pushed customers to make quick decisions. The combination of recurring subscriptions and early-bird deals helped me grow my business in a sustainable way, while keeping my clients engaged and eager to stay with me over the long term.

Offering Subscriptions and Memberships to Generate Consistent Revenue

One of the biggest challenges for any business, especially in its early stages, is generating consistent revenue. Single sales can be unpredictable, which makes it difficult to plan for future growth. That's where subscription and membership models come in.

By offering a subscription service, you're creating a reliable stream of income. Customers pay a regular fee—monthly, quarterly, or annually—in exchange for ongoing value. This model provides stability, as it ensures you have consistent revenue coming in, even if new sales slow down temporarily.

Here's why subscriptions and memberships work so well:

1. Predictable Cash Flow: With a subscription model, you know exactly how much revenue you'll be bringing in each month. This allows you to plan for expenses, reinvest in your business, and scale more predictably.

2. Increased Customer Loyalty: Customers who subscribe to your service or join a membership program are making a long-term commitment to your business. This deepens the relationship and makes it more likely that they'll stick around for the long haul, especially if they're receiving ongoing value.

3. Scalability: Subscription models can scale much faster than one-time sales because you're not starting from zero each month. As you add more subscribers, your revenue grows without the need for constant new customer acquisition.

4. Lower Customer Acquisition Costs: Once a customer subscribes, you don't need to spend as much time or money marketing to them repeatedly. Instead, you can focus on keeping them engaged and providing continuous value.

Using Early-Bird Deals to Create Urgency and Drive Sales

Early-bird deals can be a powerful tool for generating sales quickly and creating a sense of urgency around your offerings. By offering a limited-time discount or exclusive access to customers who buy early, you can encourage them to act fast and commit to your product or service before it's widely available.

Here's why early-bird deals work:

1. Scarcity Creates Urgency: When people know that something is available for a limited time or in limited quantities, they're more likely to act quickly. No one wants to miss out on a good deal. Early-bird discounts play on this fear of missing out, motivating customers to make a decision sooner rather than later.

2. Boosts Initial Sales: Early-bird deals can help you hit your sales targets faster by driving a surge of early interest. Whether you're pre-selling a product or launching a new service, offering a discount for early buyers can generate excitement and get people talking about your offering.

3. Builds Momentum for Launches: Offering early-bird deals creates buzz around your product or service launch. Early adopters become your ambassadors, sharing their positive experiences and helping you build momentum before your official launch.

In my own business, I offered early-bird deals on my coding subscription packages. For customers who signed up in the first few days, I offered discounted pricing and exclusive access to additional content. This strategy worked wonders—it helped me fill my subscription slots quickly, generated excitement around the new model, and kept customers engaged from the start.

Strategies for Pricing Your Pre-Sales, Subscriptions, and Memberships Effectively

Pricing is one of the most important decisions you'll make when offering subscriptions, memberships, or pre-sales. If your pricing is too high, you might scare away potential customers. But if it's too low, you could undervalue your product and struggle to make a profit.

Here are some strategies for pricing your offerings effectively:

1. Understand Your Costs: Before setting your prices, make sure you understand all of your costs—both fixed and variable. This

includes the cost of producing your product or service, as well as marketing, delivery, and customer support. Your pricing needs to cover these costs while leaving room for profit.

2. Offer Multiple Pricing Tiers: Customers love having options, so consider offering multiple pricing tiers. For example, you might offer a basic subscription at a lower price point and a premium subscription with added benefits for customers willing to pay more. This allows you to cater to different types of customers while maximizing your revenue.

3. Incentivize Longer Commitments: Offer discounts for customers who commit to longer subscription periods. For example, give customers the option to pay monthly, quarterly, or annually, with a discount for those who choose the annual plan. This helps improve customer retention and generates more predictable revenue.

4. Anchor Your Pricing: Use price anchoring to position your offering as a great deal. By presenting a higher-priced option next to your main product, the main option will appear more affordable by comparison. This psychological pricing strategy can help boost conversions.

Case Studies of Businesses That Used These Models for Long-Term Growth

Many successful businesses have used subscription models, memberships, and early-bird deals to fuel their long-term growth. Here are two standout examples:

1. Spotify – The Music Streaming Giant: Spotify's entire business model revolves around subscriptions. By offering both free and premium membership tiers, Spotify allows customers to experience the product before upgrading to a paid plan. The subscription model has provided Spotify with a consistent revenue stream and allowed them to invest in improving their platform, growing their user base to over 150 million premium subscribers worldwide.

2. Dollar Shave Club – Disruption Through Subscriptions: Dollar Shave Club disrupted the shaving industry by offering a subscription service for razor blades. Instead of making one-time purchases at a store, customers signed up for a monthly subscription and had razors delivered directly to their door. This model not only provided consistent revenue but also created a loyal customer base that appreciated the convenience of the service. Dollar Shave Club's success eventually led to a $1 billion acquisition by Unilever.

Both of these companies leveraged the power of recurring revenue to scale their businesses and create long-term stability. By offering subscription-based services, they were able to grow predictably and sustainably.

Key Takeaways:

• Recurring revenue models provide stability and predictability. Subscriptions and memberships create a steady stream of income that you can rely on month after month, allowing you to plan for future growth and scale more effectively.

• Early-bird deals drive urgency and help you reach early sales targets. By offering discounts or exclusive bonuses for early buyers, you can create a sense of urgency and generate excitement around your product or service launch.

• Subscriptions and memberships can turn one-time customers into long-term supporters. By providing ongoing value and nurturing relationships with your customers, you can turn one-time buyers into loyal subscribers who stick with your business over the long term.

Offering subscriptions, memberships, and early-bird deals transformed my business from a series of unpredictable sales into a well-oiled machine with consistent cash flow and a loyal customer base. These models not only provide financial stability but also deepen customer relationships, creating a sense of commitment and community around your brand. If you want to build a business that can grow sustainably over time, incorporating these recurring revenue strategies is one of the smartest moves you can make.

CHAPTER 9: BUILDING YOUR PRODUCT OR SERVICE WITH LIMITED RESOURCES

After landing my first few customers, I knew I had to step up my game. Initially, I offered basic coding lessons, but with each new student, it became clear that I needed to offer more value and improve the overall experience. I didn't have a huge budget, but I did have something just as valuable: customer cash flow. Every Rupee I earned was immediately reinvested into the business, allowing me to develop better materials, upgrade my equipment, and enhance my delivery methods.

I didn't rush to scale up too quickly. Instead, I focused on making incremental improvements based on customer feedback. This approach allowed me to keep costs low while ensuring that my lessons were getting better with every new client. By continuously reinvesting in my business and letting my customers guide me, I was able to enhance my product without taking on debt or needing outside investment.

Building Your Product or Service Incrementally Using Customer Revenue

One of the biggest mistakes new entrepreneurs make is thinking they need a fully developed product or service from day one. But the truth is, you don't need everything in place to start. In fact, some of the most successful businesses start with a minimum viable product (MVP)—the simplest version of their offering that still delivers value—and build on that incrementally as they gain customers and generate revenue.

For me, that meant starting with basic coding lessons. As more students signed up, I used their payments to invest in better materials, such as downloadable guides and exercises. I also upgraded my delivery tools by buying a new webcam to improve the quality of my live lessons. The key was that I didn't spend more than I earned. Every improvement was funded by my customers' payments, which allowed me to scale at a sustainable pace.

Here's why incremental growth works:

1. Minimizes Risk: By building your product or service slowly and using customer revenue to fund development, you minimize the risk of over-investing in something that may not work. You're not pouring money into a fully developed product upfront; instead, you're letting your customers pay for the growth of your business.

2. Allows for Flexibility: As you build your product incrementally, you can make adjustments based on customer feedback. This flexibility ensures that you're creating something that people actually want, rather than guessing what they need.

3. Promotes Sustainable Growth: You don't have to worry about scaling too quickly or taking on debt to fund your growth. By using customer revenue to drive development, you can grow at a pace that's manageable and sustainable.

Outsource Only What You Can't Do Yourself and Keep Costs Low

In the early stages of building a business, it's important to keep your costs as low as possible. For me, that meant doing most of the work myself. I created my own lesson materials, handled marketing through free tools like social media, and managed customer interactions personally. I didn't hire staff or outsource work unless it was absolutely necessary.

But as my business grew, there were certain things I couldn't do myself. For example, when it came time to create a more professional-looking website, I hired a freelance developer. But even then, I was careful about how much I spent, making sure that any outsourcing was directly tied to improving the customer experience and increasing sales.

Here are some tips for outsourcing strategically:

1. Outsource Only When Necessary: Do as much as you can yourself in the beginning. Outsource tasks that are outside your area of expertise or that would take too much time for you to do effectively. This could include things like web development, graphic design, or specialized technical work.

2. Find Cost-Effective Solutions: You don't need to hire full-time employees right away. Instead, look for freelancers or contract workers who can help you with specific tasks as needed. Platforms like Upwork, Fiverr, and Freelancer are great for finding skilled professionals at reasonable rates.

3. Focus on Value-Added Outsourcing: Only outsource tasks that will directly improve your product or service or increase your sales. For example, outsourcing the development of a high-quality website or marketing materials can help you reach more customers and generate more revenue.

Leveraging Customer Feedback to Improve Your Product

Customer feedback is one of the most valuable resources you have when building your product or service. Every piece of feedback is an opportunity to improve and refine your offering. In the early stages of my business, I made it a point to ask my students for feedback after each lesson. What did they like? What could be improved? What would they want to see in future lessons?

This feedback loop was essential. It allowed me to make improvements based on real customer needs rather than guessing what people wanted. For example, when several students mentioned that they wanted more advanced coding lessons, I used that feedback to create new materials and expand my offering. Similarly, when a few students suggested adding downloadable study guides, I used their input to create those resources.

Here's how to leverage customer feedback effectively:

1. Ask for Feedback Early and Often: Don't wait until your product or service is fully built to ask for feedback. Start gathering input from your customers as soon as possible and use it to shape your development process.

2. Listen to Your Customers: Pay close attention to what your customers are saying, especially if you hear the same feedback from multiple people. This is a sign that there's a real need or problem that you can address with your product or service.

3.Make Improvements Based on Feedback: Use the feedback you receive to make incremental improvements to your offering. This ensures that you're building something that meets your customers' needs and keeps them coming back for more.

Examples of Businesses That Built Their Products with Minimal Investment

Many successful businesses have built their products or services incrementally, using customer revenue to fund growth and avoiding the need for large upfront investments. Here are a couple of examples:

1. Basecamp – Project Management Software: Basecamp, one of the most popular project management tools, started as a side project by the founders of a web design firm. Instead of seeking outside investment, they built the product incrementally using the revenue from their design clients. As more people started using Basecamp, they reinvested that revenue into improving the product. Today, Basecamp is used by millions of people around the world, and the company has remained debt-free.

2. Warby Parker – Eyewear Retailer: Warby Parker started as a small online eyewear retailer with a simple concept: affordable, stylish glasses delivered directly to customers. Instead of building out physical stores from the beginning, Warby Parker launched as an online-only retailer, using customer sales to fund growth. Over time, they reinvested their profits into building a more comprehensive product line and eventually opening physical locations. By growing incrementally, they avoided the need for large amounts of capital and kept their overhead low.

Key Takeaways:

• Start small and build your product or service as revenue allows. You don't need a fully developed product from day one. Start with an MVP and use customer payments to fund incremental improvements.

• Outsource only when necessary and focus on reinvestment. Keep costs low by doing as much as you can yourself and outsourcing strategically. Reinvest customer revenue into areas that will directly improve your product or service.

• Customer feedback is your best guide to improving and scaling. Listen to your customers and use their feedback to refine your offering. This ensures that you're building something that meets real needs and keeps your customers coming back.

By building my business incrementally and reinvesting customer revenue, I was able to grow without taking on debt or outside investment. Every improvement I made was directly funded by my customers, which not only kept my costs low but also ensured that I was building something people actually wanted. This approach allowed me to scale sustainably, and it's a strategy that can work for you too. Start small, listen to your customers, and let their payments fuel your growth.

CHAPTER 10: CREATING A BRAND THAT CUSTOMERS LOVE

As my business began to grow, I realized that it was time to create a brand that truly resonated with my customers. It wasn't enough just to offer a good product or service—I needed to build a reputation that people could trust and recognize. But I didn't have a big budget for hiring designers or branding agencies. Instead, I focused on what my customers valued most: trust, quality, and personalized service.

I didn't try to create a brand based on flashy logos or elaborate marketing campaigns. Instead, I listened to what my customers said about their experience with me. They appreciated the fact that I was reliable, that I offered high-quality lessons, and that I made an effort to personalize my services to meet their needs. These became the core values of my brand, and I used them to build something that was authentic and deeply connected to my customers.

My strategy was simple: focus on the customer experience. Every interaction, whether through a lesson, an email, or a social media post, became an opportunity to strengthen my brand. Over time, as satisfied customers spread the word, my brand grew naturally through word-of-mouth and social media. It was built on a foundation of trust and authenticity, and it resonated with people because it was real.

The Importance of Building a Strong Brand, Even with a Small Budget

No matter how small your business is or how limited your budget may be, building a strong brand is essential to your success. Your brand is not just your logo or your website—it's the way people feel when they interact with your business. It's the reputation you build over time, through every touchpoint with your customers.

When you're just starting out, it's tempting to think that branding isn't important or that you need to wait until you can afford expensive designers or agencies. But that's not the case. Your brand can start small, and it can grow organically as your business grows. The key is to focus on the things that matter most: trust, consistency, and delivering on your promises.

Here's why building a strong brand matters, even if you're working with a small budget:

1. It Sets You Apart from Competitors: A strong brand makes your business memorable and helps you stand out from competitors. Even if your product or service isn't unique, the way you present it can be.

2. It Builds Trust and Loyalty: Customers are more likely to buy from businesses they trust. By creating a consistent and reliable brand, you build loyalty and encourage repeat business.

3. It Creates an Emotional Connection: People don't just buy products; they buy into brands. A strong brand creates an emotional connection with your customers, making them feel like they're part of something bigger than just a transaction.

4. It Grows with Your Business: Your brand is something that can grow and evolve as your business grows. Even if you start small, your brand will become more valuable over time as more people experience your product or service and spread the word.

How to Create a Brand Identity Without Hiring Expensive Designers

When I first started building my brand, I didn't have the resources to hire a branding agency or a professional designer. Instead, I focused on creating a brand identity that reflected my core values and resonated with my audience. You can do the same, even on a tight budget.

Here's how to create a strong brand identity without spending a lot of money:

1. Define Your Core Values: Start by identifying what your business stands for. What are the values that guide your decisions? For me, it was trust, quality, and personalized service. These values became the foundation of my brand, and I made sure that everything I did reflected them.

2. Know Your Audience: Understanding your customers is key to building a brand that resonates with them. What do they care about? What problems are they trying to solve? What kind of experience are they looking for? Use this insight to shape your messaging, tone, and overall brand personality.

3. Be Consistent in Your Messaging: Consistency is one of the most important elements of building a strong brand. Whether you're writing a social media post, responding to a customer inquiry, or designing your website, your messaging should always reflect your brand's values and voice. This helps create a cohesive brand identity that customers recognize and trust.

4. Use Free or Low-Cost Design Tools: You don't need expensive design software or a professional designer to create a polished look for your brand. There are plenty of free or low-cost tools like Canva, which allow you to design logos, social media graphics, and other branding materials. Keep things simple and clean—your visuals should support your brand, not overshadow it.

5. Focus on Customer Experience: Your brand is built through

the experiences your customers have with your business. Focus on delivering excellent service, responding promptly to inquiries, and making your customers feel valued. This will do more to build your brand than any logo or tagline ever could.

Building Trust and Credibility Through Consistent Messaging and Delivering on Your Promises

A great brand isn't built overnight. It's built on trust, credibility, and consistency. Every time you interact with your customers—whether through your website, social media, or customer service—you're shaping their perception of your brand. That's why it's so important to be consistent in your messaging and to always deliver on your promises.

Here are a few ways you can build trust and credibility through your brand:

1. Be Transparent: Customers appreciate honesty and transparency. Be upfront about what your product or service can and can't do. If there are delays or issues, communicate with your customers openly and let them know what to expect.

2. Deliver on Your Promises: Nothing damages a brand faster than failing to deliver on what you promise. Whether it's meeting a deadline, providing a certain level of quality, or offering a specific feature, make sure you consistently meet (or exceed) customer expectations.

3. Engage with Your Customers: Build relationships with your customers by engaging with them regularly. Respond to their questions and comments, seek feedback, and show that you're listening. This not only strengthens your brand but also fosters customer loyalty.

4. Stay True to Your Values: Your brand's values are its foundation. Every decision you make—whether it's how you handle customer service or how you price your products—should align with those values. Staying true to your values helps build credibility and trust

over time.

Examples of Bootstrapped Businesses That Built Powerful Brands

Some of the most successful brands in the world started with little to no money but were built on a strong foundation of trust, consistency, and customer experience. Here are two examples:

1. Mailchimp – Email Marketing Platform: Mailchimp started as a small bootstrapped business with a simple goal: to make email marketing easier for small businesses. Instead of spending heavily on branding or marketing, Mailchimp focused on providing excellent service and a product that worked. Over time, they built a brand that was trusted by millions of users worldwide, all without relying on outside investment. Their quirky, approachable tone and consistent customer support helped them grow into one of the most popular email marketing platforms.

2. Innocent Drinks – Smoothie Brand: Innocent Drinks started by selling smoothies at a music festival. They didn't have a big marketing budget, but they built their brand around sustainability, honesty, and transparency. By sticking to their values and delivering a product that people loved, Innocent grew into one of the UK's most beloved beverage brands. They used fun, playful messaging and packaging to create a strong emotional connection with their customers, proving that you don't need a big budget to build a brand that resonates.

Key Takeaways:

• Your brand is built through customer experiences, not big budgets. Focus on delivering value and building trust with your customers. Every interaction is an opportunity to strengthen your brand.

• Authenticity and consistency are more important than expensive branding. Be true to your values, and make sure your messaging is consistent across all channels. Customers will recognize and appreciate your authenticity.

• Listen to your customers and let them shape how your brand evolves. Pay attention to customer feedback and use it to refine your brand identity. Your customers will tell you what they value most—listen and respond.

Creating a brand that customers love doesn't require a massive budget or a fancy design team. It requires understanding your audience, staying true to your values, and delivering consistent, high-quality experiences. By focusing on trust, authenticity, and customer experience, you can build a brand that resonates deeply with your customers and grows naturally through word-of-mouth. In the end, your brand is a reflection of how you treat your customers and how well you deliver on your promises. Keep those principles at the heart of everything you do, and your brand will thrive.

CHAPTER 11: MARKETING ON A SHOESTRING BUDGET

When I first started my business, I didn't have a big marketing budget. In fact, I didn't have a marketing budget at all. But I knew that if I wanted my business to grow, I had to find a way to reach new customers. Since expensive ads and marketing agencies were out of the question, I turned to the tools I had available: social media, personal referrals, and content marketing.

I started small, posting about my coding lessons on Facebook and LinkedIn. I reached out to friends and former colleagues, offering free consultations and asking them to spread the word. Slowly but surely, my first few customers turned into more. People began recommending me to others, and word-of-mouth started to do its magic. I wasn't spending a dime, but my business was gaining traction simply because I was providing value and engaging with my audience consistently.

How to Market Your Business Without Spending a Fortune on Advertising

Marketing doesn't have to be expensive to be effective. In fact, some of the most powerful marketing strategies are free or very low-cost. When you're starting a business on a limited budget, it's essential to be resourceful and make the most of the tools available to you.

Here's how you can market your business without spending a

fortune:

1. Leverage Social Media: Social media platforms like Facebook, Instagram, LinkedIn, and Twitter are powerful tools for reaching your target audience—without any upfront cost. You can use these platforms to share valuable content, engage with potential customers, and build a following. It's important to choose the right platform for your business, where your target audience is most active.

2. Tap Into Word-of-Mouth Marketing: Word-of-mouth is one of the most effective forms of marketing, and it costs nothing. When your customers are satisfied, they're more likely to refer your business to friends, family, and colleagues. Encourage your existing customers to spread the word by offering excellent service, asking for referrals, or even creating a simple referral program where they can receive discounts or rewards for bringing in new customers.

3. Use Content Marketing: Content marketing is about creating valuable content that attracts, engages, and educates your audience. This can include blog posts, how-to guides, videos, or even social media posts. When done well, content marketing builds trust and positions you as an authority in your field, making it more likely that potential customers will come to you when they need your product or service.

4. Email Marketing: Building an email list and regularly engaging with your audience through email campaigns is one of the most cost-effective ways to stay top of mind with potential and current customers. Tools like Mailchimp or Sendinblue offer free plans that allow you to start building and nurturing your email list at no cost.

5. Collaborate with Influencers or Partner Businesses: Look for opportunities to collaborate with influencers or partner businesses that align with your target audience. These partnerships can help you reach a broader audience without a big advertising spend.

The Best Free and Low-Cost Marketing Strategies to Generate Awareness and Drive Sales

Here are some specific strategies you can use to market your business without breaking the bank:

1. Social Media Engagement:

• Regularly post on social media platforms where your target audience is active.

• Share valuable tips, stories, and behind-the-scenes content to humanize your brand.

• Respond to comments, engage with your followers, and build relationships through direct messages.

• Use relevant hashtags to increase your content's visibility and join conversations in your niche.

2. Content Marketing:

• Start a blog or create videos that showcase your expertise in your industry.

• Write posts that solve problems for your target audience, offer practical advice, or share success stories from your customers.

• Repurpose your content across different platforms (e.g., turn blog posts into infographics or social media snippets).

3. Email Marketing:

• Create a free lead magnet (e.g., an e-book, checklist, or video tutorial) to encourage people to sign up for your email list.

• Send regular email newsletters with valuable content, special offers, or updates about your business.

• Personalize your emails to make your audience feel like you're speaking directly to them.

4. Referral Program:

• Create a simple referral program that rewards customers for bringing in new business. This can be as easy as offering discounts, free products, or service upgrades to customers who refer others to your business.

5.Free Trials or Free Consultations:

• If you're offering a service, consider offering free consultations or a free trial to potential customers. This gives them a risk-free way to experience your product or service before committing, and if they're satisfied, they're likely to convert into paying customers.

Leveraging Social Media, Email Marketing, and Content to Build an Audience

When I started marketing my coding lessons, I knew that building an audience would take time and consistency. Instead of waiting for people to find me, I actively used social media, email marketing, and content creation to engage with potential customers. Here's how I did it, and how you can too:

1. Social Media:

• I posted regularly on platforms like Facebook and LinkedIn, sharing insights about coding and tips for beginners. These posts helped me establish myself as an expert in my field and attracted people who were interested in learning from me.

• I also used social media to build personal connections. By responding to comments and messages, I created a sense of community, which encouraged people to share my posts and refer me to others.

2. Email Marketing:

• As I began gaining more customers, I started collecting their email addresses to keep in touch. I sent out weekly emails with coding tips, lesson updates, and exclusive content.

• These emails kept me top of mind with my customers, and I used them to share testimonials, encourage referrals, and promote new offerings.

3. Content Marketing:

- I created simple blog posts and social media content focused on coding basics, challenges faced by beginners, and success stories from my students. This content didn't cost anything but time, and it provided real value to my audience.

- By consistently sharing helpful information, I was able to build trust with my audience. They began seeing me as someone who could help them learn to code, and many eventually signed up for my lessons.

Case Studies of Businesses That Grew Their Customer Base Using Minimal Marketing Spend

Many businesses have used free and low-cost marketing strategies to grow their customer base and achieve significant success. Here are two examples:

1. Buffer – Social Media Management Tool: Buffer, a popular social media scheduling tool, used content marketing to build their brand from the ground up. Instead of spending on ads, Buffer focused on creating blog content that provided valuable tips on social media, productivity, and startup life. This content attracted a steady stream of users, and over time, Buffer grew into a leading social media tool with millions of users—all without a large advertising budget.

2. Groupon – The Deal Giant: Groupon started with a small budget and focused on email marketing and word-of-mouth to grow their business. By offering discounts on popular products and services, Groupon was able to attract a large audience quickly. They encouraged customers to share deals with their friends, which helped them grow virally. Today, Groupon is one of the largest deal platforms in the world, but it started with simple, low-cost marketing strategies.

Key Takeaways:

- Free marketing tools like social media and email can be incredibly powerful. You don't need a big budget to grow your business—focus on using free platforms to engage with your audience and build trust.

- Word-of-mouth is a form of marketing you can generate through customer satisfaction. Deliver excellent service and encourage satisfied customers to refer others to you.

- Consistent, valuable content can build trust and attract customers organically. Whether through blog posts, videos, or social media, regularly sharing helpful content can establish your authority and draw customers to your business.

By focusing on free and low-cost marketing strategies, I was able to grow my business without spending large sums on advertising. The key was consistency, delivering value through content, and leveraging the power of word-of-mouth and social media. If you focus on building relationships and offering valuable insights, you can create a marketing strategy that helps your business thrive, no matter how tight your budget may be.

CHAPTER 12: USING CUSTOMER REVENUE TO SCALE YOUR BUSINESS

As my business continued to grow, I realized that I didn't need external investors or large loans to scale. My customers were giving me everything I needed. The revenue from my early sales provided a steady stream of cash that I could reinvest into the business. It wasn't a windfall, but it was enough to fund growth, one step at a time.

I started by using the profits to develop more advanced coding courses. As demand grew, I expanded my offerings to include more specialized lessons and began considering how I could scale without taking on unnecessary risk. Instead of jumping into hiring a large team or investing in expensive infrastructure, I stayed lean and flexible. I hired only when it was absolutely necessary, bringing on a small team to manage the increasing workload. By keeping the business lean and relying on customer revenue, I was able to grow sustainably and maintain full control over the direction of my company.

How to Use the Revenue from Your First Sales to Scale Your Business Step by Step

One of the most effective ways to scale your business without taking on debt or outside investment is to reinvest the profits from your early sales. This strategy allows you to grow gradually, using the revenue generated by your customers to fund each new phase of development. It's a slower, but much more sustainable, path to growth.

Here's how to scale your business using customer revenue:

1. Reinvest Profits into Product Development: In the early stages, I focused on improving my product—the coding lessons. As I earned money from my first few students, I reinvested that cash into creating more advanced lessons and expanding the curriculum. This allowed me to offer a more comprehensive product without needing to borrow money or seek external funding. If you can continually improve your product or service based on customer feedback, you'll not only keep your current customers happy, but you'll also attract new ones.

2. Expand Your Offerings Gradually: Once you've developed a core product or service that your customers love, think about ways to expand your offerings. In my case, I started with beginner coding lessons, but as demand grew, I expanded into advanced courses and even personalized tutoring. Each expansion was funded by customer revenue, allowing me to test new ideas without overextending my resources. Look for natural extensions of your business that complement your existing offerings and serve your customers in new ways.

3. Stay Lean: One of the biggest mistakes growing businesses make is trying to scale too quickly, which can lead to overextending resources and taking on unnecessary risks. Instead, focus on staying lean. Only hire when absolutely necessary, and avoid spending money on unnecessary overhead. In my case, I hired a small team when the workload became too much for me to handle alone, but I was careful to bring on people who added real value to the business. By keeping your operations lean, you'll have more flexibility to adjust as you grow and avoid the pitfalls of over-expansion.

4. Automate and Outsource Where Possible: As your business

grows, you'll reach a point where you can't do everything yourself. Instead of hiring full-time employees for every task, consider automating processes or outsourcing specific tasks to freelancers. This helps you keep costs down while still growing efficiently. For example, I used automated tools for scheduling lessons and managing my email list, which saved me time and allowed me to focus on delivering value to my students.

Strategies for Expanding Your Product Line or Services Using Customer Cash Flow

Scaling a business doesn't mean you have to take on massive risks or jump into unfamiliar territory. By leveraging customer revenue, you can grow your product line or services organically and sustainably. Here are a few strategies to consider when expanding your business:

1. Test New Offerings Before Fully Committing: Before fully developing a new product or service, test it with your existing customer base. Offer it as a pilot program or pre-sell it to gauge interest. This allows you to validate the demand without committing a large amount of resources upfront. If it's successful, you can then use the revenue from the initial sales to fund the full launch. This approach worked for me when I introduced more advanced coding courses—I started with a small group of students, then expanded based on their feedback and the revenue generated from the initial lessons.

2. Offer Upsells or Add-Ons: Another effective way to scale is by offering upsells or add-ons to your existing customers. These could be premium versions of your product, additional services, or complementary products that enhance the customer experience. Upselling to your current customer base is often easier and more cost-effective than acquiring new customers. In my case, I offered personalized one-on-one tutoring sessions as an upsell to students who wanted more tailored support.

3. Expand Into New Markets: Once you've established a strong

customer base in one market, consider expanding into new markets. This could mean reaching new geographic regions, targeting different customer segments, or introducing your product to a new industry. However, it's important to approach this carefully—use the revenue from your existing business to fund the expansion and make sure you fully understand the new market before diving in.

The Importance of Staying Lean and Flexible as Your Business Grows

One of the key lessons I've learned throughout my journey is the importance of staying lean and flexible as your business scales. Growth can be exciting, but it can also be risky if not managed properly. By keeping your business lean, you maintain the flexibility to pivot when necessary and avoid taking on too much overhead too quickly.

Here's why staying lean is so important:

1. Reduces Financial Risk: Scaling too quickly can lead to cash flow issues, especially if you're spending more than you're earning. By staying lean, you minimize your financial risk and avoid taking on unnecessary debt.

2. Allows for Flexibility: Business environments change quickly, and the ability to pivot or adjust your strategy is crucial. When you have a lean operation, it's easier to adapt to changing market conditions or customer needs without being weighed down by excess costs or large teams.

3. Keeps You Focused on What Matters: Staying lean forces you to focus on the most important aspects of your business—your customers and your product. By avoiding unnecessary distractions or costs, you can dedicate more time and resources to delivering value and driving growth.

Examples of Businesses That Scaled Organically Without Needing

Outside Investment

Many successful businesses have scaled organically, using customer revenue to fuel their growth. Here are a couple of examples:

1. Basecamp – Project Management Software: Basecamp, one of the most popular project management tools, scaled without taking on outside investment. The founders focused on building a great product, growing their customer base organically, and reinvesting profits to expand the business. By staying lean and avoiding debt, Basecamp was able to grow sustainably and remain in full control of their company.

2. Mailchimp – Email Marketing Platform: Mailchimp is another example of a company that scaled without external funding. They started small, offering email marketing services to small businesses, and grew gradually by reinvesting customer revenue into product development and marketing. Today, Mailchimp is a leading email marketing platform, all built through organic growth and customer-funded revenue.

Key Takeaways:

• Scaling doesn't require a massive infusion of cash; it requires reinvestment of profits. By using customer revenue to fund your growth, you can expand your business organically and sustainably without taking on debt or outside investment.

• Stay lean and flexible as you scale to avoid overextending your resources. Keep your operations streamlined, hire only when necessary, and focus on automation and outsourcing to keep costs down.

• Customer-funded growth is sustainable and keeps you in control of your business. By relying on customer revenue to scale, you retain full control over your company and avoid the pressures of external investors or lenders.

Scaling a business doesn't have to involve massive risks or large injections of capital. By focusing on reinvesting customer revenue, staying lean, and expanding strategically, you can grow your business sustainably while keeping full control. My journey has shown me that slow, steady growth—fueled by the trust and support of your customers—leads to long-term success. Stay true to your values, focus on delivering value, and let your customers guide you as you scale.

CHAPTER 13: TURNING CUSTOMERS INTO ADVOCATES AND BRAND AMBASSADORS

One of the most rewarding parts of my entrepreneurial journey was watching my customers become advocates for my business. They weren't just satisfied with my services—they were excited to share them with others. I noticed early on that many of my new clients came from referrals, and this word-of-mouth marketing became a powerful engine for my growth. My customers were my biggest fans, and they became the best marketers for my business.

To capitalize on this, I built a simple referral program that rewarded customers for bringing in new business. It wasn't a complicated or expensive system, but it made a huge difference. I offered discounts or free services to customers who referred friends or colleagues, and in return, they spread the word. This organic growth strategy was not only cost-effective but also built stronger relationships with my existing clients. They felt like they were part of my business's success, and their loyalty only deepened.

How to Turn Satisfied Customers into Loyal Advocates Who Promote Your Business

Satisfied customers are one of your most valuable assets. When people are happy with your product or service, they're more likely to tell others about it, and personal recommendations carry a lot of weight. Turning satisfied customers into advocates doesn't happen by accident—it's the result of consistently delivering value, building trust, and engaging with your audience in meaningful ways.

Here's how you can turn your customers into loyal advocates:

1. Deliver Exceptional Service: The foundation of customer advocacy is satisfaction. If you want your customers to spread the word about your business, you need to consistently exceed their expectations. This means delivering high-quality products, providing excellent customer service, and addressing any issues promptly and professionally.

2. Stay Engaged: Don't disappear after the sale. Keep in touch with your customers through regular communication, whether that's via email, social media, or direct follow-ups. Show genuine interest in their feedback and make them feel valued. When customers feel like they have a personal connection with your business, they're more likely to advocate for it.

3. Personalize the Experience: Tailoring your products or services to meet the specific needs of your customers can go a long way in turning them into loyal advocates. People appreciate businesses that understand their unique challenges and go the extra mile to solve them. Personalization makes your customers feel special, increasing their likelihood of recommending you to others.

4. Celebrate Your Customers: Publicly recognize and celebrate your customers' achievements or loyalty. Whether it's through social media shoutouts, customer spotlights, or loyalty awards, showing appreciation reinforces the emotional connection between your customers and your brand. The more valued they feel, the more likely they'll be to spread the word.

Building a Referral Program That Rewards Customers for Bringing in New Business

One of the most effective ways to incentivize customer advocacy is by implementing a referral program. This is a structured way to encourage your existing customers to refer new business to you by offering rewards or incentives in return. It's a win-win situation: your customers get rewarded for their loyalty, and you get new customers at a fraction of the cost of traditional marketing.

Here's how to build a simple, effective referral program:

1. Offer Meaningful Rewards: Your referral rewards should be valuable enough to motivate customers to participate. These could be discounts, free products, or even exclusive services. For my coding lessons, I offered free sessions or discounted rates to customers who referred new students. The rewards don't have to be extravagant—what's important is that they're meaningful to your customers.

2. Make It Easy to Participate: Your referral program should be simple and easy to use. Make sure your customers know how to refer others, and provide them with clear instructions and referral codes or links. The easier it is for customers to refer others, the more likely they'll be to do it.

3. Track and Measure Results: Implement a system to track referrals and ensure that both the referrer and the new customer receive their rewards. You can use referral software or a simple spreadsheet to keep track of who's referring whom. This helps you identify your top advocates and ensures that your program is working as intended.

4. Promote Your Program: Don't assume your customers will automatically know about your referral program—actively promote it through your email campaigns, social media, and customer communications. Make sure it's a visible part of your marketing strategy so that customers are constantly reminded of the benefits of referring others.

Leveraging Word-of-Mouth Marketing to Grow Your Customer Base Organically

Word-of-mouth marketing is one of the most powerful growth drivers for any business. When people hear about a product or service from someone they trust, they're much more likely to try it themselves. The best part? Word-of-mouth marketing is free and incredibly effective.

Here's how to leverage word-of-mouth marketing to grow your customer base:

1. Encourage Reviews and Testimonials: Positive reviews and testimonials from happy customers can significantly influence potential buyers. Encourage your customers to leave reviews on platforms like Google, Yelp, or industry-specific sites. Share these testimonials on your website and social media to build trust with new prospects.

2. Create Shareable Content: Content marketing isn't just about blog posts or videos—it's about creating content that people want to share with others. Whether it's a helpful guide, an inspiring customer story, or a fun behind-the-scenes look at your business, shareable content can expand your reach and get more eyes on your brand.

3. Engage in Online Communities: If your business serves a niche market, find online communities where your target audience is active. Participate in discussions, offer advice, and build relationships without being overly promotional. People will naturally start referring others to your business once they see you as a valuable resource.

4. Delight Your Customers: Go above and beyond to deliver memorable experiences. Whether it's through surprise discounts, handwritten thank-you notes, or simply offering stellar customer service, these small gestures make a big impact and encourage customers to spread the word.

Examples of Businesses That Grew Through Customer Referrals and Advocacy

Many successful businesses have harnessed the power of customer advocacy and referrals to grow their customer base without spending large amounts on advertising. Here are two examples:

1. Dropbox – File Sharing Service: Dropbox famously used a referral program to grow its user base quickly. They offered extra storage space to both the referrer and the new user, incentivizing people to share Dropbox with their friends. This strategy was hugely successful and helped Dropbox grow from 100,000 users to over 4 million in just 15 months. The simplicity of their referral program and the value of the reward (extra storage) made it easy for people to participate.

2. Tesla – Electric Cars: Tesla leveraged its passionate customer base to grow through a referral program that offered rewards such as free charging, discounts, and even early access to new products. Tesla's loyal customers became brand ambassadors, spreading the word about the company's products to friends and family, helping Tesla grow rapidly without relying on traditional advertising.

Key Takeaways:

• Satisfied customers are your best marketing tool. Happy customers naturally want to share their positive experiences with others, and personal recommendations are far more powerful than traditional ads.

• Referral programs incentivize growth through word-of-mouth. Offering rewards for referrals encourages your customers to actively promote your business and helps you grow your customer base without spending heavily on marketing.

• Building a community around your product ensures long-term loyalty and organic growth. When customers feel like they're part of your brand's journey, they're more likely to stick around, refer others, and become your biggest advocates.

Turning customers into advocates and brand ambassadors is one of the most effective ways to grow your business organically. When people love your product or service, they naturally want to share it with others. By focusing on customer satisfaction, creating a simple referral program, and leveraging word-of-mouth marketing, you can build a community of loyal advocates who will help you grow your business—without needing to spend heavily on traditional marketing. In the end, the best growth comes from those who believe in your brand and are excited to help you succeed.

CHAPTER 14: LEVERAGING CUSTOMER FEEDBACK TO DRIVE INNOVATION

As my business grew, it became clear that listening to my customers was one of the most powerful tools I had. Early on, I had relied on feedback to refine my coding lessons, but as my customer base expanded, their input became even more critical. I made it a point to ask my customers what they needed, what they liked, and, most importantly, what could be improved. This consistent feedback loop kept my customers engaged and helped me stay ahead of their evolving needs.

One example that sticks out is when several of my students expressed interest in more specialized coding topics, such as mobile app development. I hadn't initially planned to offer such courses, but their feedback showed me that there was a demand for it. So, I developed an advanced course on mobile app coding, and it quickly became one of my most popular offerings. Without listening to my customers, I might have missed that opportunity to innovate and grow.

How to Use Customer Feedback to Continuously Improve and Innovate Your Product or Service

Customer feedback is a goldmine of insights that can help you refine your current offerings and develop new ones that better serve your audience. The key is to create a system that allows you to gather, analyze, and act on that feedback consistently.

Here's how to use customer feedback to drive continuous improvement and innovation:

1. Make It Easy for Customers to Provide Feedback: If you want valuable input from your customers, you need to make it as easy as possible for them to share their thoughts. This can be done through surveys, follow-up emails, social media polls, or even direct conversations. The more accessible your feedback channels are, the more insights you'll gather. For example, I often sent out short surveys to my students after each lesson, asking them what they liked, what they didn't, and what they wanted to learn next.

2. Listen to What Your Customers Are Saying (and Not Saying): Sometimes, the most valuable feedback isn't the glowing reviews, but the constructive criticism. Pay attention to what your customers are telling you, but also read between the lines. If customers are consistently asking for a certain feature or service, or if they're not returning after trying your product, it's a sign that something needs to be improved. Negative feedback is not a setback—it's an opportunity to get better.

3. Create a Feedback Loop: A feedback loop is a process in which customer input leads to actionable changes, and those changes are then communicated back to the customers. This shows your customers that you're listening to them and making improvements based on their suggestions. For example, when I launched the mobile app development course based on student feedback, I made sure to thank those who suggested it and let them know that their input had directly influenced the new offering.

4. Act on Feedback Quickly: Customers want to see that their feedback is making a difference. Once you gather insights, act on them as soon as possible. Whether it's making small tweaks to your product or developing a completely new service, responding to feedback in a timely manner demonstrates that you value your

customers' opinions.

Creating a Feedback Loop That Keeps Customers Engaged and Invested in Your Success

One of the most effective ways to keep customers engaged with your brand is by creating a feedback loop that involves them in your decision-making process. When customers see that their opinions are driving real changes, they become more invested in your business and more loyal to your brand.

Here's how to create a successful feedback loop:

1. Ask for Feedback Regularly: Don't wait until there's a problem to ask for feedback. Make it a regular part of your customer interactions. After every purchase, service, or interaction, ask your customers how you did and what you can do better. For my business, I consistently asked students for input at the end of each course, which helped me keep a pulse on their needs.

2. Acknowledge and Act on Feedback: When customers take the time to give you feedback, let them know that you've heard them. If their suggestions lead to real changes, let them know how their input influenced your decisions. This acknowledgment shows customers that you value their opinions and are committed to improving their experience.

3. Close the Loop: After making changes based on customer feedback, follow up with your customers to show them the results. This could be an email explaining the improvements you've made or a public announcement on social media. Closing the loop reinforces the connection between customer feedback and your actions, keeping your audience engaged and loyal.

How to Turn Criticism into Opportunities for Growth and Innovation

No business is immune to criticism, but how you respond to that criticism can make all the difference. Instead of seeing negative feedback as a failure, view it as a roadmap for improvement. Some of the best innovations come from addressing customer pain points and frustrations.

Here's how to turn criticism into an opportunity for growth:

1. Welcome Negative Feedback: While it's nice to receive praise, negative feedback is often more valuable. It highlights the areas where your business can improve and gives you direct insight into what isn't working. When students mentioned that they wanted more interactive exercises in my lessons, I didn't take it as a personal failure—I took it as a challenge to improve my curriculum.

2. Respond Constructively: When you receive criticism, respond with an open mind and a solution-oriented attitude. Acknowledge the customer's concerns and let them know how you plan to address the issue. For example, when some of my students struggled with certain aspects of the coding lessons, I offered additional support through one-on-one sessions to help them succeed.

3. Innovate Based on Feedback: Use customer criticism as a catalyst for innovation. If multiple customers are highlighting the same issue, it's a sign that something needs to change. Don't be afraid to pivot or make significant improvements if necessary. Many successful businesses have made major changes based on customer feedback and thrived because of it.

Examples of Businesses That Pivoted or Improved Based on Customer Feedback

Many businesses have used customer feedback to pivot or significantly improve their products, resulting in greater success. Here are a couple of notable examples:

1. Slack – Communication Tool: Slack started as an internal communication tool for a game development company. After receiving feedback from users, the founders realized that the tool

itself had broader potential beyond gaming. They pivoted to focus on Slack as a communication platform for businesses, and it's now one of the most widely used collaboration tools in the world. This shift was driven by listening to customer needs and recognizing an opportunity to pivot.

2. Netflix – Streaming Service: Netflix originally started as a DVD rental service. As customer preferences shifted toward streaming content online, Netflix listened and innovated its business model. They transitioned from mailing DVDs to offering an online streaming service, revolutionizing the way people consumed media. This pivot, based largely on customer feedback and evolving market trends, helped Netflix grow into a global entertainment giant.

Key Takeaways:

• Listening to customers is key to driving innovation and staying ahead of the competition. Your customers know what they want—pay attention to their feedback, and use it to improve your product or service.

• A feedback loop keeps customers engaged and ensures you're meeting their needs. Regularly asking for and acting on feedback shows customers that you value their input, which fosters loyalty and trust.

• Constructive criticism is a valuable tool for improving your business. Don't fear negative feedback—embrace it as an opportunity to innovate and make your product or service even better.

Leveraging customer feedback has been one of the most important drivers of innovation in my business. By listening closely to what my customers needed, I was able to stay ahead of the competition and continuously improve my offerings. Whether it's refining a current product, launching something new, or pivoting entirely, customer feedback is the key to long-term success. Stay open, stay engaged, and let your customers guide you toward growth and innovation.

CHAPTER 15: STAYING PROFITABLE WITHOUT TAKING ON DEBT OR INVESTORS

As my business continued to grow, one of the things I was most proud of was that I had managed to do it all without taking on debt or external investors. Every step of the journey had been funded by my customers, and every expansion, every new product offering, and every hire was the result of careful financial planning and reinvestment of profits. By staying lean, managing cash flow diligently, and reinvesting wisely, I was able to maintain profitability while staying in complete control of my business.

I wasn't beholden to outside investors, and I didn't have to worry about paying back loans. Instead, I grew at a pace that suited my business and my customers. This freedom allowed me to focus on building something sustainable, without the added pressure of meeting investor demands or the stress of paying down debt.

How to Maintain Profitability as Your Business Grows Without Taking on External Funding

Growing a business without external funding is entirely possible, but it requires discipline and a careful approach to managing your finances. The key is to reinvest profits strategically and manage your cash flow effectively so you can scale sustainably. Here's how to do it:

1. Focus on Customer-Funded Growth: Like I did with my coding lessons, you can grow your business by using revenue from your early customers to fund your expansion. Whether it's improving your product, hiring a small team, or expanding your marketing efforts, focus on growing at a pace that your profits can support.

2. Reinvest Profits Wisely: Instead of relying on loans or investors to fund growth, reinvest your profits strategically. This could mean upgrading your equipment, developing new product offerings, or hiring additional staff. The key is to reinvest in ways that directly contribute to your business's ability to generate more revenue, creating a positive feedback loop of growth.

3. Stay Lean: One of the biggest risks of rapid growth is taking on too much overhead too quickly. By staying lean—keeping your operations streamlined, outsourcing where possible, and avoiding unnecessary expenses—you can scale at a sustainable pace without needing to take on debt or give up equity.

4. Prioritize Profitability Over Rapid Growth: It's tempting to grow as fast as possible, but if profitability takes a backseat to growth, you risk running into cash flow problems. Focus on building a profitable business first and foremost, and let growth follow from there. For me, this meant taking a steady approach, expanding only when the cash flow was strong enough to support it.

Managing Cash Flow, Budgeting, and Financial Planning for Long-Term Sustainability

Cash flow management is one of the most critical aspects of running a debt-free business. It's not enough to generate sales—you need to make sure your business has enough cash on hand to cover expenses, pay your team, and invest in future growth. By mastering cash flow management, budgeting, and financial planning, you can ensure your business remains profitable and sustainable in the long term.

Here are some practical tips for managing cash flow effectively:

1. Keep Track of Cash Flow Regularly: Regularly monitor your business's cash flow—know what's coming in, what's going out, and when payments are due. Tools like accounting software or even simple spreadsheets can help you stay on top of this. Understanding your cash flow patterns allows you to anticipate any shortfalls and plan accordingly.

2. Create a Budget and Stick to It: Developing a budget is essential for staying profitable and avoiding unnecessary expenses. Plan your spending based on your expected revenue and prioritize expenses that directly contribute to growth, such as marketing or product development. Be disciplined about sticking to your budget to prevent overspending.

3. Build a Cash Reserve: One of the best ways to protect your business against unforeseen challenges is to build a cash reserve. This buffer will give you peace of mind and financial flexibility, allowing you to handle slow periods or unexpected costs without taking on debt.

4. Negotiate Payment Terms: If your business relies on vendors or suppliers, consider negotiating favorable payment terms that improve your cash flow. For example, ask for longer payment terms from suppliers while offering early payment discounts to your customers. This can create a cash flow cushion, giving you more breathing room.

Why Avoiding Debt and Dilution Keeps You in Control of Your Business

Staying debt-free and avoiding outside investors isn't just about financial security—it's about maintaining control over your business. When you take on debt, you introduce financial pressure to meet repayment obligations, which can stifle your ability to make long-term decisions. Similarly, bringing on investors often means giving up equity and control, which can lead to decisions that prioritize short-term returns over long-term sustainability.

Here's why staying debt-free and avoiding dilution is so

important:

1. Freedom to Grow at Your Own Pace: Without the pressure of meeting investor expectations or repaying loans, you're free to grow your business at a pace that makes sense for you and your customers. This allows you to focus on building a sustainable business that prioritizes long-term success.

2. Full Control Over Decision-Making: When you avoid giving up equity to investors, you retain full control over your business decisions. This means you can stay true to your vision and values, without being swayed by external pressures.

3. Less Financial Stress: Running a business is stressful enough without the added burden of debt repayments or investor demands. By staying debt-free, you reduce the financial pressure and create a more stable foundation for growth.

Examples of Businesses That Scaled Successfully While Staying Debt-Free

Many successful businesses have scaled while staying debt-free and maintaining full control over their operations. Here are a couple of examples:

1. Spanx – Shapewear Brand: Spanx founder Sara Blakely started her company with just $5,000 of her own savings and refused to take on external funding. She grew the business organically by reinvesting profits and staying lean. Today, Spanx is a global brand, and Blakely owns 100% of the company, giving her full control over its direction.

2. Patagonia – Outdoor Apparel: Patagonia has maintained its commitment to sustainability and ethical business practices by avoiding debt and outside investors. Founder Yvon Chouinard grew the company through reinvestment, ensuring that profits were used to support the company's values and long-term goals. This approach has allowed Patagonia to scale globally while staying true to its mission.

Key Takeaways:

• Profitability and sustainability go hand-in-hand when you rely on customer funding. By focusing on reinvesting profits and managing cash flow, you can scale your business without taking on debt or external investors.

• Careful cash flow management is key to long-term success. Monitor your cash flow regularly, create a budget, and build a cash reserve to ensure your business remains financially stable as it grows.

• Staying debt-free keeps you in control and reduces financial pressure. Avoiding debt and dilution allows you to grow at your own pace and maintain full control over your business decisions.

Building a profitable, sustainable business without relying on debt or external investors is entirely achievable. By focusing on customer-funded growth, managing your cash flow carefully, and reinvesting profits strategically, you can scale your business on your own terms. For me, this approach has allowed me to maintain full control, avoid financial stress, and build a business that's not only successful but sustainable for the long term. Staying debt-free has given me the freedom to make decisions that align with my vision, ensuring that my business grows at a pace that's both profitable and manageable.

CHAPTER 16: BUILDING A BUSINESS THAT CAN THRIVE IN ANY ECONOMY

Over the years, I've witnessed the ebb and flow of the economy, watching businesses rise during booms and collapse during downturns. What became clear to me is that those who rely heavily on external funding or rigid business models struggle the most when things go south. In contrast, my customer-funded approach not only kept me afloat during challenging times but also allowed me to grow, no matter the economic climate.

Even when the market was uncertain, my customers continued to support my business. By staying adaptable, diversifying my offerings, and keeping my operations lean, I built a business that could weather economic storms. My customers were my strength, and by constantly listening to their needs, I was able to pivot and adjust my strategies to keep moving forward.

How to Build a Resilient Business That Can Survive Market Downturns or Economic Shifts

Economic downturns are inevitable, and how your business responds to them can determine its long-term survival. A business built on a solid foundation of customer funding, adaptability, and diversification is more likely to thrive, even when the economy takes a hit. Here's how to build resilience into your business model:

1. Diversify Your Revenue Streams: Relying on a single product or service can leave your business vulnerable during tough times. By diversifying your offerings, you spread your risk and create multiple revenue streams, ensuring that if one area of your business is affected, others can continue to generate income. For example, when demand for basic coding lessons began to plateau, I introduced more specialized courses, tutoring sessions, and digital resources. This diversification helped me reach new customers and sustain revenue even during economic slowdowns.

2. Keep Your Business Lean and Agile: Flexibility is key to navigating economic uncertainty. By keeping your operations lean and avoiding unnecessary expenses, you can pivot quickly when needed. In my case, I always maintained a small, efficient team and outsourced tasks only when necessary. This kept overhead low and allowed me to make swift changes without disrupting my business.

3. Prioritize Cash Flow Management: Cash flow is the lifeblood of any business, and during economic downturns, it becomes even more critical. Careful cash flow management ensures that you have the liquidity to cover expenses and invest in new opportunities when they arise. Building a cash reserve during good times can give you a financial cushion during leaner periods, reducing your reliance on external funding.

4. Listen to Your Customers and Stay Adaptable: Your customers are your best resource for surviving economic shifts. By staying in tune with their changing needs, you can adapt your offerings to match current demands. For example, during one economic downturn, I noticed that customers were more hesitant to invest in long-term coding programs. In response, I introduced shorter, more affordable courses, which allowed me to continue generating revenue while providing value to my customers.

Diversifying Your Revenue Streams and Minimizing Risks to Stay Profitable in Any Economy

Diversification is one of the most effective strategies for building a business that can withstand economic shifts. By offering a range of products or services, you reduce your dependency on any one source of income, which minimizes your risk and creates more stability. Here's how to diversify your revenue streams:

1. Expand Your Offerings: Look for opportunities to expand your product or service line in ways that complement your core business. For example, after establishing my coding lessons, I introduced advanced courses, one-on-one coaching, and digital resources like e-books and tutorials. Each new offering catered to a different customer segment, increasing my revenue streams while minimizing risk.

2. Introduce Recurring Revenue Models: Subscription models, memberships, and retainer agreements create a steady stream of recurring revenue, which can help stabilize your income during economic fluctuations. For instance, I introduced subscription-based services that offered ongoing support and advanced lessons to students. These recurring payments provided a predictable cash flow, giving my business greater financial stability.

3. Target Multiple Markets: Don't limit yourself to one target market. By expanding into different customer segments or geographic markets, you can spread your risk and increase your potential for growth. When I started offering courses for both beginners and advanced students, I diversified my audience and was less vulnerable to shifts in demand from any one group.

4. Balance Short-Term and Long-Term Revenue: A healthy mix of short-term sales and long-term contracts can help you weather economic volatility. Short-term sales provide immediate cash flow, while long-term contracts or subscriptions offer financial security over time. This balance ensures that you have the flexibility to adjust to market conditions while maintaining a

stable income.

Future-Proofing Your Business with Innovation and Adaptability

The most resilient businesses are those that can adapt to change and continuously innovate. By staying ahead of market trends and listening to your customers, you can ensure that your business remains relevant and profitable, regardless of external conditions. Here's how to future-proof your business:

1. Embrace Innovation: Always be on the lookout for new technologies, processes, or ideas that can improve your business. Whether it's automating certain tasks, adopting new marketing strategies, or offering new digital products, innovation can keep your business competitive and responsive to changes in the market.

2. Stay Flexible: Flexibility is key to surviving economic shifts. Build a business that can pivot quickly when necessary. Whether that means shifting your product offerings, adjusting pricing, or even targeting new markets, staying flexible allows you to respond to changes in customer behavior or the broader economy.

3. Invest in Continuous Learning: The most successful businesses are those that never stop learning. Stay curious about new industry trends, market opportunities, and customer needs. By constantly seeking new knowledge and staying informed about your industry, you position your business to thrive in the future.

4. Build Strong Customer Relationships: Customers are the backbone of any successful business, and strong relationships with them can provide a steady source of revenue during difficult times. Stay engaged with your customers, seek their feedback, and continue providing value. Loyal customers will support your business through thick and thin, helping you weather economic challenges.

Examples of Businesses That Thrived During Economic

Challenges by Staying Customer-Funded

Many businesses have successfully navigated economic downturns by relying on customer funding, diversification, and adaptability. Here are two examples:

1. Airbnb – Home Rental Platform: During the 2008 financial crisis, Airbnb was still a fledgling company. Rather than seeking outside investors, the founders used their own resources and customer payments to keep the business running. By offering affordable alternatives to traditional lodging, they found a niche market during the economic downturn. Today, Airbnb is one of the largest home rental platforms globally, and its customer-funded growth helped it thrive during a challenging economic period.

2. Mailchimp – Email Marketing Platform: Mailchimp started as a bootstrapped business and grew without external funding. During the 2008 recession, they stayed agile and responsive to customer needs, introducing freemium models and expanding their service offerings. By listening to their customers and adapting their product to the needs of small businesses during tough times, Mailchimp thrived while others struggled.

Key Takeaways:

- A diversified revenue model ensures long-term stability. By offering a range of products and services, you spread your risk and create multiple streams of income, reducing your vulnerability to economic fluctuations.

- Customer funding allows you to stay flexible and adaptable in any economic climate. When your business is funded by your customers rather than external investors or debt, you have the freedom to pivot quickly and make decisions that align with market demands.

- Resilience comes from building a business that can evolve with market conditions. By embracing innovation, staying flexible, and continuously learning, you position your business to thrive no matter what the economy throws your way.

Building a business that can thrive in any economy is about more than just surviving tough times—it's about creating a foundation of resilience, adaptability, and innovation. By staying customer-funded, diversifying your offerings, and remaining agile, you can navigate economic downturns and come out stronger on the other side. In the end, a business built on these principles can not only survive, but thrive, no matter what the future holds.

EPILOGUE

Epilogue for Start Now, Pay Later: Building a Business with Your Customers' Money

As we reach the conclusion of this book, I hope you now see that building a successful business doesn't require deep pockets, an angel investor, or a massive initial investment. The customer-funded model is not just a concept—it's a proven, actionable approach that has worked for countless entrepreneurs, including myself.

The journey of starting and growing a business is rarely linear. It is full of unexpected challenges, risks, and rewards. What sets apart the successful entrepreneurs is their ability to adapt, persevere, and turn obstacles into opportunities. This book has given you the tools to do just that.

By leveraging the power of your customers, you're not just raising funds—you're validating your idea, building loyalty, and creating a community that believes in your business as much as you do. These principles are designed to empower you to take the leap, to innovate, and to grow, regardless of where you start or how much capital you have.

This journey is yours to shape. Whether you are launching your first venture or scaling your existing business, remember that every step forward, no matter how small, is a step toward your goals. It's not about where you start, but about the value you create for your customers along the way.

As you embark on this exciting path, don't be afraid to reach out, share your successes, or ask for help when needed. The business community thrives when we learn from and support each other, and I encourage you to stay connected, stay inspired, and continue growing.

Thank you for taking the time to explore these strategies and insights. I look forward to hearing your success stories and seeing how you use these concepts to build your business, your way.

Here's to your success—may you always start small, think big, and let your customers guide you to greatness.

Haroon Kareem

AFTERWORD

Afterword for Start Now, Pay Later: Building a Business with Your Customers' Money

As I look back on the journey of writing this book, I'm reminded of the very principles I've shared with you throughout these pages: start with what you have, learn as you go, and let your customers guide you. This philosophy has shaped not only my businesses but also my life, and I'm humbled to be able to share these insights with you.

Writing this book has been more than just documenting a strategy—it's been about sharing a mindset. The customer-funded model isn't just a technique; it's a way of thinking that challenges traditional ideas about how businesses are started and scaled. By embracing this model, you're stepping into a realm where creativity, resourcefulness, and your relationship with your customers take center stage.

If you've made it this far, I hope you've come to see that starting a business isn't about waiting for the perfect moment or securing the perfect investor. It's about taking action with the resources you have right now and building your dream piece by piece. Your customers are your most valuable asset, and when you harness their belief in your vision, you unlock a powerful path forward.

For me, building multiple companies with this model has been a profound experience. The lessons I've learned along the way have not only shaped my businesses but have also redefined my approach to life. Challenges will always arise, but with the right mindset and strategies, they can be transformed into opportunities.

To those of you embarking on your entrepreneurial journey or scaling your existing business, I hope this book serves as a roadmap and an inspiration. You now have the tools to take your next steps with confidence, knowing that you don't need everything to be perfect—you just need to start. Your customers will help you get where you need to go.

Thank you for letting me be a part of your journey. Remember: it's not about the size of your investment; it's about the value you create and the relationships you build along the way. I look forward to hearing your success stories and seeing how you bring these ideas to life.

Here's to your continued success—keep thinking big, taking action, and letting your customers be your guide.

Haroon Kareem

ACKNOWLEDGEMENT

First and foremost, I want to acknowledge Mathew Abraham, my dear friend and the person who played a pivotal role in my transformation. From a communist mindset to becoming an ex-communist and an entrepreneur, my journey would have been vastly different without Mathew's guidance and unwavering support. His influence has shaped my entrepreneurial spirit and helped me see the potential in building a business that empowers others.

I also extend my deepest gratitude to Sunil Pezhunkad, my high school teacher, who taught me that blindness is not a limitation but an opportunity. His words of encouragement, reminding me that I could achieve anything despite my challenges, gave me the confidence to push forward, even when the road was tough.

To my customers and clients, whose trust and loyalty have been the backbone of my business. Your feedback, support, and belief in what I offer have helped me shape and grow my ventures. Without you, none of this would have been possible.

Finally, to the countless colleagues, mentors, and friends who have provided advice, encouragement, and inspiration along the way—thank you. This book is as much a reflection of your support as it is of my own journey. Your words and wisdom have fueled my growth, and I am forever grateful for the role each of you has played in my life and business.

Thank you all for being part of my story.

ABOUT THE AUTHOR

Haroon Kareem

Haroon Kareem: A Global Visionary in Business Development and Corporate Strategy

Mr. Haroon Kareem is a distinguished global entrepreneur, business consultant, and a transformative leader renowned for his innovative approach to business and corporate growth. Born in Kerala, India, and fully visually impaired, Mr. Kareem's remarkable journey from humble beginnings to international success exemplifies resilience, leadership, and the power of technology.

With a career spanning continents, Mr. Kareem has delivered

hundreds of presentations worldwide, advising on business development, corporate strategy, and turnaround solutions. His guidance has led numerous companies across the globe—from startups to established enterprises—out of challenging times and into sustainable profitability. His clientele spans Europe, the USA, the UK, the Middle East, India, and beyond, reflecting the global impact of his expertise.

At just 16 years old, Mr. Kareem launched his first business with a mere 799 Indian Rupees, Less than 10 $, teaching coding online. His unconventional approach—funding his growth through his customers—became the foundation of his entrepreneurial philosophy, which he has since applied to guiding countless entrepreneurs toward success. This belief in customer-funded growth is central to his strategy, enabling businesses to scale with minimal initial investment.

Mr. Kareem's academic credentials are equally impressive. He is an alumnus of Harvard Business School (Class of 2022) and holds degrees from the University of the People in California, the University of Manchester, and the University of Edinburgh in the UK. His well-rounded educational background equips him to provide multifaceted consultancy services, from digital transformation to business model innovation.

In 2024, Mr. Kareem made history by becoming the first fully visually impaired entrepreneur to incorporate and successfully operate a company in the UAE. His company, Webiniser FZE, based in Ajman Free Zone, specializes in IT consultancy, business strategy, HR solutions, and management consultancy. Alongside Webiniser Ltd in the UK, a firm renowned for its AI-driven solutions and digital transformation services, Mr. Kareem continues to lead the charge in helping businesses navigate the complex global market.

A passionate advocate for accessibility, Mr. Kareem founded Global Accessibility Ltd, an organization focused on developing assistive technologies for the visually impaired. His work empowers individuals with disabilities by offering innovative solutions that enhance their ability to thrive in the digital world.

This reflects his long-held belief that technology can be a force for equality, giving everyone, regardless of physical challenges, the tools to achieve independence and success.

Mr. Kareem's leadership also extends to his other ventures, including TheWebSchool, a professional development platform, and TheWebPublishers, a digital media company. Additionally, his AI startup, TheWebIntelligence, is making waves with its advanced automation products designed to drive efficiency across multiple industries.

Despite his extraordinary achievements, Mr. Kareem's vision for the future remains expansive. His goal is to further globalize his businesses, foster international collaborations, and continue driving innovation. He stands as a mentor to entrepreneurs worldwide, proving that no challenge—whether personal or professional—can stand in the way of success with the right mindset and strategy.

Mr. Kareem's journey redefines the boundaries of entrepreneurship, particularly in the context of accessibility. His message is clear: Start small, think big, and let your customers guide you. Through his book, Mr. Kareem aims to inspire entrepreneurs everywhere, showing them that the key to success lies not in the initial investment, but in the value created for customers.

www.ingramcontent.com/pod-product-compliance
Lightning Source LLC
Chambersburg PA
CBHW070152230526
45471CB00002B/633